CONTROL SELF-ASSESSMENT

A Guide to Facilitation-Based Consulting

CONTROL SELF-ASSESSMENT

A Guide to Facilitation-Based Consulting

Richard P. Tritter

JOHN WILEY & SONS, INC.

New York • Chichester • Weinheim • Brisbane • Singapore • Toronto

Copyright © 2000 by John Wiley & Sons, Inc. All rights reserved.

Published by John Wiley & Sons, Inc.

Published simultaneously in Canada.

This publication is designed to provide accurate and authoritative information in regard to the subject matter covered. It is sold with the understanding that the publisher is not engaged in rendering legal, accounting, or other professional services. If legal advice or other expert assistance is required, the services of a competent professional person should be sought.

Designations used by companies to distinguish their products are often claimed as trademarks. In all instances where John Wiley & Sons, Inc., is aware of a claim, the product names appear in initial capital or all capital letters. Readers, however, should contact the appropriate companies for more complete information regarding trademarks and registration.

Library of Congress Cataloging-in-Publication Data:

Tritter, Richard P.
  Control self-assessment : a guide to facilitation-based consulting / Richard P. Tritter.
      p.   cm.
  Includes index.
  ISBN 0-471-29842-5 (cl. : alk. paper)
  1. Control self-assessment (Auditing) 2. Management Consulting—Analysis. 3. Business process improvement—Evaluation.
I. Title.
HF5667.3.T75 2000
657'.45—dc21   99-39995
                                                                        CIP

10 9 8 7 6 5 4

Contents

Contents

Contents

Contents

Contents

About the Author

Richard Tritter has had a lengthy career consulting in strategic planning and business systems development, strategic marketing, and business process improvement. He has been director of a Big-Five self-assessment practice, worldwide, which conducted facilitated meetings with groups of client executives at the vice-presidential level and higher. These sessions developed corporate business, information and marketing strategies, as well as business process improvement plans.

Earlier, Dick led engagements in strategic planning and information needs, as well as marketing and sales planning, while with this firm. His clients came from financial services, public utilities, manufacturing, healthcare, education, construction, and numerous other industries. He is a certified trainer of computer-supported group consulting techniques, and has trained consultants in the United States, Canada, Scotland, Mauritius, Australia, New Zealand, Hungary, and the United Kingdom. Dick was cowinner of the Massachusetts Better Government Competition in 1991, awarded by Governor William Weld, for his facilitation work in improving adult handicapped programs.

In his former high-technology career, Dick was responsible for conceiving and developing three new software systems at Digital

Equipment Corp., and later managing their positioning, marketing strategies, and sales campaigns. In that role, Dick conceived and created the computing industry's first independently tested retail software product, with testing conducted by KPMG Peat Marwick. The out-of-the-box quality of that software gave it immediate market leadership, and a highly profitable product life. Later, Dick's technology career focused on horizontal marketing approaches—using partnerships and strategic alliances to gain sales and market share.

Dick is a highly regarded international authority on Control Self-Assessment, the most recent and most advanced facilitated consulting technique. In 1994, he wrote an internal guide to Control Self-Assessment for his consulting firm. In 1995, he researched and authored an international study of this methodology for the Institute of Internal Auditors, entitled *Control Self-Assessment—Experience, Current Thinking and Best Practices*. This book, his third on CSA, is a "how-to" book for those interested in implementing various CSA success techniques—for internal auditing, management consulting, business process improvement, and risk management.

Preface

In 1991, I joined a Big Five (then Big Eight) accounting firm as a consultant to help in the development of their facilitation consulting methodology. Although I had some past experience in encounter groups—both as participant and leader—I had yet to see a generalized technique of open-forum discussions that could achieve specific business objectives.

True, I had helped conduct a few strategic marketing/planning sessions with a previous employer, but these could be viewed as coincidental successes. After all, can one expect to have a two-year marketing plan developed in only three hours? A plan that is agreed and supported by all participants? And followed with little variation for the entire program life cycle, with full success? Such results must be anomalies, and could not possibly be achieved with predictable regularity—or could they?

Initially I focused on smaller consulting engagements, where minimal consulting time meant choosing between thorough system planning and profitability—*using traditional techniques*. Therefore, a new approach had to be invented, which would be the ideal combination—"better, cheaper, and faster."

At first, we focused facilitative techniques on developing strategic plans, information systems plans, and other forms of *future* planning meetings. All these techniques were based on the creative-thinking techniques of the 1970s and 1980s, helping groups to "think out of the box" and to gain consensus in the plans they developed. The first methodology, developed by Dr. George Land of Leadership 2000, Inc. (Scottsdale, Arizona), delivered excellent results for Dr. Land, but lesser results for others. It therefore became necessary to break the process down to its component parts, to analyze their successes and failures, and to try to make the techniques explainable and replicable for any trained facilitator.

In later years, I served as an external consultant to the same firm, to help research a new facilitative technique developed by the internal auditing profession. That technique, "Control Self-Assessment" (CSA), took an entirely different approach to facilitated group discussion. It looked at the present status of business processes and analyzed what worked, what didn't work, and how to fix it. This was a major departure from the strategic planning facilitation—CSA looked at *present* facts, not future possibilities. Although there were many different CSA techniques, there was a common thread to them all—a core process that could be applied generally, and with predictable outcomes. Clearly, this was a winning consulting methodology.

The use of facilitation is now well-proven, both for future-planning uses and present-process analysis. These concepts are simple, but somewhat different from traditional decision-making methods. Facilitative consulting is psychologically based to enroll the meeting's participants, and then to resolve the specific problem at hand; in contrast, traditional methods are factually based to get to the "right answer," and then to get people's agreement to this approach afterward—without their participation in making the decision, initially.

Which works better? See for yourself. Read the first few chapters, and then experiment in your own department meetings. I believe that you will find that participative decision-making has a more complete analysis of facts, is supported better by the participants, and has better long-term results. It also takes significantly less time.

While learning these methodologies, feel free to experiment. Facilitation is in its early phase of development, and could use more conceptual models to cover different types of situations. The main skills required are an open mind, a desire to help others achieve their best possible results, and a belief that "pulling information" from people can work better than "pushing decisions" onto them.

Acknowledgments

In 1991, I first met Dr. George Land, CEO of Leadership 2000, Inc. He had new ideas and, most importantly, a formal and replicable facilitation process that could be depended upon to give excellent results. His associate, Tom McNamee, invented and developed the Conexus® voting system for Leadership 2000—a software and hardware application that in many ways is still ahead of the competition, five years later. I learned the depths of facilitation and the importance of electronic voting systems—particularly in achieving success with difficult areas of discussion. I thank them for that education.

I would also like to thank Professor Bob Bostrom of the University of Georgia Department of Management, and Vikki Clawson, Ph.D., his former student, for their permission to reprint "The 12 Dimensions of Effective Facilitation." As a piece of original research, this list codifies the skills and responsibilities needed to achieve success in the field of electronic facilitation.

Most importantly, I would like to extend my sincerest thanks and deepest acknowledgement to Bruce Raby, former General Auditor of the Export Development Corporation, a Crown corporation in Ottawa, Canada. Bruce was the original framer of the research study that I authored for the IIA Research Foundation, entitled *Control Self-Assessment—Experience, Current Thinking and Best Practices*. It was Bruce's vision, insight, patience, and hard work—both in developing the original research plan, and in working the many agendas that were required behind the scenes—that assured the success of that study in 1996. Bruce is always thoughtful in his dealings, remained true to the original vision of the Ottawa IIA Chapter's Research Committee, and greatly increased the quality of the finished work. I learned greatly from his professionalism.

Many thanks are separately owed to the Institute of Internal Auditors for their support and encouragement in these efforts to document Control Self-Assessment, both here and in the work mentioned above. They have also published two of my articles in the *CSA Sentinel,* a magazine devoted to the study and improvement of Control Self-Assessment techniques; these appear as Chapters 8 and 10 of this book. Finally, they have granted copyright permission for various content in this book, for which I am deeply grateful.

1

Facilitative Consulting and Control Self-Assessment: An Introduction

FACILITATIVE CONSULTING: A BRIEF HISTORY

The historical development of modern facilitation methods started with group psychological techniques during the 1960s. At that time, the Esalen Institute expanded the use of traditional group therapy into "group encounters," where the psychological issues of individuals were examined (and even acted out) in front of the other participants. This was a powerful technique in advancing individuals' understanding of their own problems. It also started a group-meeting approach to studying difficult issues.

The Esalen techniques have become further developed by psychology professionals. The interesting point for business readers, however, is that these approaches later moved into the business world. Starting in the 1970s, many businesses tried to take advantage of the candor and high information flow that characterized these methods.

○ First, many corporations sent executives to weekend or week-long retreats, where the encounter group approach was expected to help managers understand themselves better and then, it was hoped, to become better at managing others. An unexpected result of these retreats, however, was that many managers did "find themselves," went back to their work environment, and resigned to pursue other interests. Therefore, encounter groups experienced only a short period of popularity in business.

o Next, a number of human resources professionals started using group techniques as team-building exercises. Often these sessions were combined with "experiential learning," typically an outdoor course involved elements of controlled risk, group interaction, and individual challenge. Examples included ropes courses, pole climbing, and group survival expeditions into difficult terrain. In each experience, individuals learned to extend themselves into the unfamiliar and uncomfortable and often returned with a greater sense of confidence that helped improve their interactions with others. Such courses continue today and are considered beneficial in a general sense. The difficult question, however, is whether the corporate sponsor achieves specific value from the courses, value that could justify the investment of time and money. The results often were general and could not be shown to create specific improvement.

o The third phase was the application of team-building techniques to team problem-solving approaches. In these courses, sample exercises were presented that could be solved only through involvement of numerous members of the team. In this way, participants learned to depend more on others, and on the harnessing of numerous participants' knowledge and effort.

In a separate but parallel development, the 1970s and 1980s saw the expanding use of "work circles" in the manufacturing industries, especially automotive. First used widely in Sweden, work circles discarded the linear assembly line and replaced it with groups of workers assembling the car as a joint task. The results of this integrated approach were beneficial to many parties:

- o Workers derived greater job satisfaction.
- o Employers were better able to retain experienced workers.
- o Work circles developed numerous improvements in the assembly process.
- o The automobile end customer purchased a more reliable vehicle.

Although the use of work circles has had limited application in American car manufacturing, its success in European companies helped advance the involvement of workers in the improvement of their own work process. This, in turn, helped advance the development of consulting techniques that were based on participants' own knowledge.

By the mid-1980s, consultative techniques focused on developing and increasing individuals' creative potential: coming up with new ideas to solve old problems. Although these efforts initially did not target specific problems, they did improve many business managers' ability to see situations differently, and to develop unconventional approaches that would help their departments to succeed.

At this point, the stage was set for harnessing these group techniques into a well-structured business consulting methodology. This book describes the development of one such methodology.

TRADITIONAL VERSUS FACILITATIVE CONSULTING

Any business plan is best accomplished when the work team itself has created it and supports it. That is the basic tenet of all facilitative consulting—that its results are derived from the stakeholders themselves, not from outside "experts." The core premise of facilitation is that the participants (the work team) are the true experts for the business process they perform daily. Of course, in many special situations, outside expertise may be needed—but only when specific gaps in client knowledge become apparent. The core knowledge of the process, the problem situation, and the potential solution usually reside in employees and management who are affected by the issues under examination.

That premise, however, is in some ways opposite to traditional consulting techniques. The eight steps of traditional consulting, usually based on outside expertise, are typically as follows:

1. A team of experts in the business process is gathered.
2. The team then interviews clients in key positions relative to the issues posed. Typically, interviews are conducted on a one-on-one basis: stakeholder and outside consultant.
3. The consulting team gathers, reviews, and discusses all interview results.
4. The consultants develop a problem-resolution plan, often with key client input, because:
   a. Clients may have information that "fills in the gaps."
   b. More important, clients' involvement will help in gaining acceptance of the eventual plan.
5. Consultants then present the plan to the broader client group, typically in a presentation attended by both consultants and clients.
6. Frequently, the proposed plan does not satisfy the clients as a group and has to be revised significantly. This is due to differences between individual knowledge and the group's more complete knowledge, when assembled together.
7. The plan revision loop continues until the final "expert plan" is accepted.
8. Implementation then ensues.

The above process is a time-honored approach. What has become clear in recent years, however, is that this approach is time-consuming and may ultimately be ineffective—particularly in dealing with rapidly changing issues. Many companies have gone through this traditional approach and later remember the project's results as "the consultants' plan, which we never fully implemented."

What went wrong? Why was there never full implementation? The answer lies more in human psychology than in business school analysis: The plan that was proposed, revised, and eventually accepted was the outsiders' plan, not that of the true stakeholders in the business process. As a result, none of the client management team ever felt true ownership in its successful implementation, even though all members had been interviewed at the beginning and were presented with the plan at the end of the engagement. This lack of true, personal involvement hinders acceptance and implementation of any outside experts' consulting recommendations.

In contrast, facilitative consulting follows a simpler approach:

1. A smaller consulting team is gathered. This includes:
   o a lead facilitator
   o a cofacilitator for session planning, as well as recording sessions and operating voting systems
   o traditional consultants to help frame the issues for the facilitator (optional)
   o a subject-matter expert in cases of highly technical discussions (optional)
2. The team meets with the key client to understand the issue under study and to define key priorities in developing the eventual solution (e.g., profitability, safety, simplification of business process, etc.).
3. The traditional consulting team does some background research, but only a fraction of the traditional, full-interview effort described earlier.
4. The traditional team provides the results to the facilitator and the assistant, who then develop a facilitation plan that will obtain the required information and will develop the desired results.
5. The facilitation session is held with all, or nearly all, business stakeholders attending.
6. The plan resulting from this stakeholders' session is written up by the consultants and presented to the client.

7. Implementation then follows, based on the client consensus that was developed during the meeting.

Although the second description seems nearly as complex as the traditional approach, it is far simpler in practice. First, the amount of information gathered prior to the facilitation session—the centerpiece of the process—is far less than the traditional series of one-on-one interviews. Second, clients themselves develop information and data into a working plan, with the assistance of the facilitator, during the facilitation session(s). These sessions are intensely focused and elicit clients' individual and group knowledge to understand and solve the problem.

That is the key difference between traditional and facilitative consulting: not just the process used to develop a plan, but the source of the ideas within. Which plan is "better"—the outside experts' plan or the inside stakeholders' plan? The answer to that question depends on who may be responding. In any case, the vital question is critical to all consulting clients: Which plan will be *implemented?* That is easy to answer: the plan that the clients have developed themselves, with the active assistance of the facilitative consulting team. When stakeholders themselves solve a problem and build a plan for implementation, they will support that effort.

To see the advantages of the facilitation approach, besides the obvious plus of having a plan developed by the clients themselves, see Exhibit 1.1. This exhibit reviews the process diagrams of the two different approaches to strategic planning engagements.

The sample agenda for a facilitated approach is far more effective and time-saving than the traditional approach. In essence, that methodology gets to a final plan by repeated interviews, gaining greater buy-in by revising the expert plan. The facilitation methodology, however, obviates this multiple-loop effort by having all the clients in one room at the same time, forging agreement through in-depth discussion of the issues and their potential solutions. The efficiency gain is dramatic, and the quality and implementability of the plan are also increased.

Exhibit 1.1   Traditional versus Facilitative Consulting Approaches

Traditional:

1. Interview Clients   2. Consultants Form Plan   3. Present Plan to Clients   4. Design, Build, Implement   5. Success

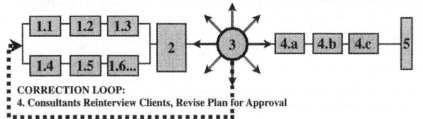

CORRECTION LOOP:
4. Consultants Reinterview Clients, Revise Plan for Approval

Facilitative:

1. Facilitate Plan with All Clients   2. Consultants Design, Build, and Implement   3. Successful Project

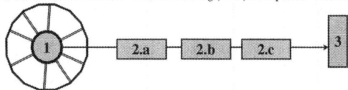

WHY SHOULD BUSINESS MANAGERS, CONSULTANTS, AND AUDITORS BE INTERESTED?

The facilitative approach to consulting presents a radically new method for obtaining information, developing new perspectives on the business process, and resolving problems that are deep-rooted in the organization. The key to this approach is the gathering of all stakeholders in a single location to discuss the issues. As the discussion evolves, participants not only contribute their own knowledge but also hear and integrate the facts and opinions expressed by all others concerned.

By the latter half of the meeting, the participants understand the problem better—and from many different perspectives besides their own. Plan development occurs at this point, when a group perspective has evolved through the in-depth discussions of the early phase of the meeting. Note that a group perspective never fully evolves in the traditional consulting approach, and only partially emerges in the group presentation of the consultants' expert plan.

The facilitative approach is based on certain foundational beliefs:

- Clients are the true experts of the business process under study, due to their day-to-day involvement with it.
- Only by being together and discussing the issues together can a true, multiperspective understanding of the subject matter develop.
- Once a full understanding exists within the group, the development of a plan for action will be efficient, all-encompassing, and supported by the members involved in its development. Thereafter, they typically will support the plan and help enroll others in the implementation process.

Finally, the facilitative approach is highly efficient: Once the meeting starts, most problems will have initial solution strategies in place within four to six hours. Occasionally, more sessions are required, but not often. The plan that participants develop is often an "80/20" plan; an accurate, top-down solution that needs further detail to make it implementable throughout the organization. But the development of the initial approach from a top-down perspective is critical, since the session is based on the entire group of participants sharing their perspective and understanding of the problem. Speed and efficiency, plus the ongoing support of the participants during the implementation phase, are what have made the facilitative approach so successful. The speed of this process is so remarkable that it can cause a significant drop in engagement fees for the outside consulting firms; as a result, facilitation has had only limited growth among consulting firms.

STRATEGIC PLANNING AND CSA

To best understand Control Self-Assessment, or CSA, it is necessary to understand that prior forms of facilitative consulting were oriented to developing a *future plan*—that is, bringing the participants from a present/problem orientation to a future/solution orientation. The psychological side of that facilitative style took participants from a discussion of their problems or issues through a multistep discussion that elevated their perspectives on the issues. The final stage was for participants to see their organization or project in a "future perfect" perspective: imagining the situation to be solved and bringing success to the client organization. At this point, the facilitator would ask participants to "look back from this picture of perfect success" and describe the ideas that "enabled [notice the past tense] that success to be achieved." From this perspective, many new ideas would emerge, because the participants were no longer seeing the current problem situation.

All facilitated planning sessions involve the development of a "future perfect" view of the problem. This requires a lengthy facilitation effort, where the facilitator acts as a guide for the group, aligning their comments and bringing them to new and higher perspectives on the issues. It also requires that the facilitator have significant psychological skills, since raising perspectives can be a difficult process. Exhibit 1.2 provides a sample agenda that illustrates a typical facilitated strategic planning session.

In 1987 three innovative professionals at Gulf Resources Canada, Ltd. (Calgary, Alberta), devised a new approach to conducting internal audits. Paul Makosz, Tim Leech, and Bruce McCuaig experimented with interviewing groups of employees simultaneously in a facilitated session, seeking to determine where audit or process controls were strong or weak, and to devise improvements for those controls. They named the new approach Control Self-Assessment (CSA) and found that it was highly effective in conducting numerous departmental audits across a large corporation. In later years, as demands for strengthening internal controls increased due to the financial debacles of the 1980s, CSA became an accepted method for quickly getting at the root of control weaknesses.

Controls were not, however, the sole application of the CSA technique. The same approach was equally good for finding out the details of specific problems in any business process,

Exhibit 1.2   Sample Strategic Planning Facilitation Session

Setting ABC Corp.'s Future Direction
Agenda—Day One

8:00 A.M.   **Breakfast**

8:15   **Meeting Convened**

8:30   **Introduction: Meeting Objectives**

FACILITATION PROCESS:

STEP 1: Participants introduce themselves, relate their own desired outcomes for the day's meeting.

STEP 2: Problem Discussion—Detailing current business process areas that have difficulty and need improvement.

STEP 3: Environmental Scan to describe:
> Obstacles—Detailing the forces that prevent resolution of problems
> Enablers—List those forces that will help bring about resolution of problems

10:00 A.M.–10:15 A.M.   Morning Break

STEP 4: Creative Idea Generation—Focusing on the group's future vision for the company, participants list ideas that enabled them to achieve their business mission or will solve problems. Ideas are then grouped into key strategies and discussed.

12:00 noon–1:00 P.M.   Lunch

STEP 5: Vote strategic profile map—Using key strategies/issues developed in step 4, participants electronically vote on current performance and importance of each key strategy/issue.
- Interpret map as to group's average position for each strategy.
- Interpret map as to scatter diagrams' meaning re consensus.

2:00 P.M.   Tactical Breakout Sessions
Group discusses implementing tactics for key issues/strategies, as follows:
- Collect all ideas from entire meeting, categorize and understand them.
- Affinity-group ideas within each topic, then list the topic's major themes.
- Discuss these ideas, add their own.
- Develop recommendations to main meeting for how to accomplish this strategy.
- Fill out Tactical Planning Form for each specific tactic recommended.

3:30 P.M   Afternoon Break

3:45   Meeting Reconvenes

Group presents their strategies, tactics, and job tickets. Participants listen, discuss, and leave meeting understanding all recommended strategies and tactics.

5:00 P.M.   First Day's Meeting Concludes

Agenda—Day Two

8:00 A.M.   **Breakfast**

8:15   **Meeting Convened**

8:30   **Presentation: Results of First Day's Session**

9:00   **Detailed Planning for Top-Ranked Tactics**

10:00 A.M.   **Morning Break**

10:15 A.M.   **Resume Tactical Planning**

11:00 A.M.   **Review Final Tactical Plans**
                Vote on Group's Consensus on Strategic/Tactical Plans
                Prepare for Second Meeting with Middle Management

12:00 noon   **Strategic Planning Meeting Concludes**

continues

Exhibit 1.2   Continued

TACTICAL PLANNING FORM

Key Strategy: _____

Description of Tactic: _____

_____

_____

Person(s) Responsible: _____

Special Resources or Skills Required?

Person-weeks:_____   Investment Required: $_____

Special Skills: _____

Outsourceable?   Yes:_____   No:_____   Comments:_____

Action Steps and Milestones:

_____

_____

_____

Performance Measures:

_____

_____

---

determining the likely causes of those problems, and suggesting solutions or improvements. In addition, the definition of "controls" broadened widely in the 1990s, so that a control is now seen as anything that assists a company or its employees in achieving their objectives—in other words, anything that can improve business or job performance. This is the larger application of CSA and the reason that it promises to go far beyond the internal audit profession and touch all forms of business consulting and business management.

CONTROL SELF-ASSESSMENT VERSUS
THE STRATEGIC PLAN

The single greatest change that occurred when the CSA approach was developed was to use facilitation to elicit participants' knowledge about *present-day facts and issues*. In effect, a CSA facilitation is a polite interrogation of the group, asking questions in the present tense and finding present-day causes of problems. Even the potential solutions gleaned from a CSA session are not future-perfect strategies; rather, they are suggestions and ideas that come from the stakeholders' existing ideas about the situation. No elevation of perspective is required, and therefore the task facing the facilitator and requisite skills are less demanding. This means that CSA facilitations are easier to conduct than the strategic plan, and CSA facilitators are easier to find and train. The sessions are also more businesslike and more comfortable for business participants. To illustrate the differences in CSA, a sample CSA agenda is shown in Exhibit 1.3.

Notice that the CSA approach is more direct in achieving its results than the strategic planning methodology. That is because CSA is simply trying to find out what the participants know, not what they can imagine. This is the strength of the self-assessment technique and also its particular attraction for internal auditors. For the general consulting community and for business management, however, this is also a key benefit that was not available before the development of CSA: getting to "the truth" from the multiple perspectives of all involved clients, quickly and easily.

IMPROVING BUSINESS PERFORMANCE WITH
CONTROL SELF-ASSESSMENT

In recent decades, the view of business as a collection of activities has developed into a view of an integrated business process, or series of processes, focused on achieving corporate objectives. Management consulting now focuses on these processes, breaking them down into subprocesses where necessary and seeing where they work well or poorly together. Numerous overlying processes are involved in a typical enterprise—manufacturing, finance, human

Exhibit 1.3 Sample CSA Session Agenda (See Chapter 4 for Subject Matter Description)

XYZ Engine Rebuilders Co.

Control Self-Assessment Meeting

Meeting Agenda

Meeting Starts at 9:00 A.M.

Breaks will be as follows:
   10:00 **Morning Break: 15 minutes**
   12:00 **Lunch: 30 minutes**
   3:00 **Afternoon Break: 15 minutes**

I. Welcome and Introduction
   A. Logistics of Today's Meeting
   B. Project Objectives
   C. Today's Meeting Objectives
   D. Risk Survey Results

II. Overview of Meeting Process
   A. Risk Categorization
   B. Questions for Each Risk
   C. Voting Techniques

III. Discussion and Voting of Business Risks
   A. Engine Business Risks
   B. Components Business Risks
   C. Fuel System and Electrics Business Risks
   D. Core Logistics Business Risks
   E. Logistics Operation Business Risks
   F. General Business Risks

IV. Voting Comparison of Business Unit Risk

V. Conclusion
   A. Questions Regarding Process
   B. Next Steps

Meeting Concludes at 4:00 P.M.

---

resources, and so on. The difficulty in the past has been to find a consultative method that is suited to the process view of business, since more traditional tools still look at singular activities.

   CSA is ideally suited to this use. Because of its flexibility, it can be tuned to look at an enterprise in any number of ways. There is the vertical study of a company or department, such as bringing an entire department together (management through clerical staff) to review and improve its operations. There is the horizontal view, where a single level of management is gathered to look at the company as a whole. Finally, CSA even can address diagonal processes, such as the success or failure of a companywide/top-to-bottom Total Quality Initiative. Flexibility and this process-based approach enable CSA to be used to improve any aspect of business performance. This fits well with the view that "controls" apply very broadly in today's business environment—they go far beyond the usual financial control definition of the past, into any area where a process needs to be defined and regulated to ensure its proper operation.

CONTROLLING BUSINESS RISKS WITH CONTROL SELF-ASSESSMENT

Another modern development has been the study of business risks to help guide corporate success. In this area, a business risk is anything that threatens achievement of business objectives. Such risks could be environmental, such as the strength of the national economy; here the issue is to ensure that the enterprise is able to adjust well to such risks occurring, even though they are outside the company's control. The majority of business risks, however, are internal. They include possibilities of catastrophic events, poor communication between departments, failure to retain key employees, and so on. Business risks can easily be analyzed in CSA sessions, and proper solutions can be put in place to strengthen the company's responses to them.

The CSA tool is used most often to study whether tasks are being performed successfully or not and to understand business risks.

Through CSA, the stakeholders themselves determine what the problems or risks are, what the causes are, and what possible solutions might be applied. In the long term, this is expected to be the greatest value CSA provides to users—a flexible, real-time, fast-reaction tool for solving business problems and addressing business risks.

BASICS OF CONTROL SELF-ASSESSMENT

In conducting a CSA inquiry, a basic question format is repeated in all discussion segments. Question formats will be adapted to each

CSA session and will vary depending on the objectives to be achieved. In Exhibit 1.3, for example, an engine rebuilding process is broken down into the following segments:

o Engine business risks
o Components business risks
o Fuel system and electrics business risks
o Core logistics business risks
o Logistics operation business risks
o General business risks

Each of these areas provides a well-defined discussion area, one that enables participants to go into specific detail regarding problems encountered and possible solutions. Note that these topics are specific to the manufacturing industry but could be altered to fit the financial process, the internal audit process, the product development process, and so on, with equally valid results.

To find out the desired information, specific questions need to be developed in cooperation with the key client's needs. These might include:

o What are the elements of this business process? How are they accomplished?
o What are the strengths of the process? Where is it working well?
o *Where are there difficulties or problems in the process?*
o What are your suggestions to solve these problems?

In a company where there are numerous "silos" that do not communicate well with each other, another question could be added to provide specific emphasis:

o What types of cooperation are needed across departments to ensure that these improvements will succeed?

Notice that we have shown above the basic design of a CSA session. This is the second of two requirements in establishing a CSA methodology:

○ Define the segments of discussion that can be addressed in detail, each requiring a one- to one-and-a-half-hour discussion.
○ Define the key questions that can be applied across all segments.

Although there is a lot more to designing a proper CSA approach for a given issue, these two elements always form the core planning effort. Later chapters provide more details to address issues of depth of information versus breadth, dealing with multiple-dimension issues, time limitations, and so on, but these elements will always be the key design issues.

The actual conduct of the CSA meeting is based on the segments and questions. The facilitator acts as the group interviewer, asking each question until the group's input is exhausted or has satisfied the information needed. During each question-and-answer segment, the behavioral dynamic is that while one person is making a comment, all other participants are hearing it and comparing it to their own experience. As a result, all but the simplest questions will generate numerous answers from different stakeholders, and often a full discussion of the issue will ensue. These discussions are a key benefit of CSA sessions and should not be cut out or reduced in importance. Clients will obtain far greater value from the discussion than from *n* numbers of interviews because the participants are not only contributing their own knowledge, *they are also reacting to the different information contributed by others.* This provides an excellent feedback to the client sponsor, to the participants themselves, and to the facilitator. These discussions lead to the oft-repeated participant comment, "This has been the most informative/educational meeting I have ever attended."

Additionally, CSA and other facilitation-based methodologies are natural communication vehicles between departments. When a meeting is held involving all those concerned with a specific issue or process, their discussion naturally brings out existing gaps in communication, cooperation, and understanding between departments. One of the most immediate benefits of CSA, therefore, is that it brings out issues and control weaknesses between independent working groups or departments—the "white spaces" of the organizational chart.

MEETING MECHANICS

Once the core segments and questions have been planned and the participants have been invited, the session itself is relatively simple to conduct. Experienced facilitators will find that the "polite interrogation" approach is simpler than other facilitation forms, and the detail of the answers is typically excellent. Recording of the results is no longer done with flipchart sheets mounted on the wall, rather, the cofacilitator makes a transcript using a computer and word processing software. The transcribed text can be projected onto a screen throughout the meeting, enabling participants to review the wording recorded from their statements and to correct the record in real-time mode.

Participants quickly become comfortable with this style of transcription, but the real benefit of the projection is far more valuable to the facilitator. By projecting the questions to be asked, the discussion is much easier to keep on track. Participants see the most recent comments, see the questions to be asked next, and will nearly always keep their comments within the desired scope and subject matter.

CSA meetings can be tiring, both for the facilitator and the participants. This is due to the psychological effect of discussing business issues in minute detail and generally discussing them from a negative viewpoint. In contrast, strategic planning meetings may last much longer but typically leave participants energized: This is due to the creative effort and positivity of a meeting that develop strategic solutions in a comfortable, informal setting. After an excellent strategic planning session, a facilitator sometimes receives applause from the participants. Unfortunately, this is not the case with CSA. Two factor will balance the session's underlying negativity: the facilitator's skill at lightening the mood, and the business value of the result. In today's business climate, most companies prefer the more immediate and more actionable benefits of CSA results to those of a strategic planning engagement.

ELECTRONIC SCRIBING AND VOTING SYSTEMS

No discussion of CSA can be complete without an understanding of electronic voting systems and the value they provide. Although electronic scribing and voting could be considered optional for a CSA meeting, both should be seriously considered to make the meeting achieve its greatest value.

Electronic scribing provides an immediate transcript of the meeting, one that can even be handed out at the end of the meeting in rough-draft form. That is convenient, to be sure, but it also provides a record of comments that all participants have tacitly approved. There is little possibility that the comments will be retracted or revised at a later time, when they have already been projected for participants to see and correct. This greatly eliminates the situation of participants "misspeaking themselves," as one famous politician once phrased it. For further information on electronic scribing, see the exhibit on this subject in Chapter 10. The transcript also provides specific detail for management's review, helping them to better understand the problem situation and recommendations.

The use of electronic voting can provide extraordinary value to a CSA session and client report. Fundamentally, electronic voting systems enable the consulting team to quantify participants' perceptions of the issues, and their preferences and priorities for solutions. This seems a tall order for those unfamiliar with these systems, but it is commonly done when electronic voting systems are available.

To ensure that electronic voting is used to maximum effectiveness, the design of the votes must be integrated with the objectives of the CSA session and the consulting engagement. Although the voting "maps" may seem complex, they are actually simple to understand and to construct for specific purposes. There are only a few basics to understand before building a voting map.

First, there are two different types of voting responses, scale voting and pair comparison voting. In *scale voting*, participants vote on a 1-to-*n* scale (1 to 7, 1 to 9, etc.) to indicate their degree of preference. This is a quick way to vote but only brings out the voters' conscious preferences; often it shows what is "safe" from an organizational view. There are two other weaknesses to this style of voting: It can be manipulated consciously, and voters can vote the same score for numerous items.

In *pair comparison voting*, participants compare a set of choices with each other, voting all possible combinations of pairs to construct a matrix of preference choices. This type of voting takes much longer, but its strength is that it develops a set of priorities that are subconscious and deeply held by the participants. Each single voter will be able to see his or her own true preferences, as opposed to the "politically correct" choices revealed by scale voting. (Individual maps are distributed privately and confidentially.) In addition, the average of all individual votes will bring out the entire group's deeply held values and priorities.

Second, votes can be combined into one-, two-, or three-dimensional maps. The most useful are the two-dimensional maps, for they are easy to understand at a glance. One-dimensional maps provide little depth and insight, and three-dimensional maps are often too complex for the participant group to understand easily.

Third, it is necessary to design a template for interpretation for each type of map used. The top-left quadrant may be the highest-priority project in some maps, but it may also indicate a lack of sufficient controls in another map. See Exhibits 1.4, 1.5, and 1.6 for examples of these maps.

Notice that each map has axes chosen specifically to fit the objectives of the sessions, and each map has its own interpretation template and voting style. The visual effect of these maps in a facilitation session is dramatic, for it immediately shows the thinking of the group as a whole and gives participants insight on how their thinking may differ from the group's. Even more effective are the individuals' voting maps, available from only a few voting systems, which are handed out confidentially to ensure

Exhibit 1.4   Sample Strategic Map

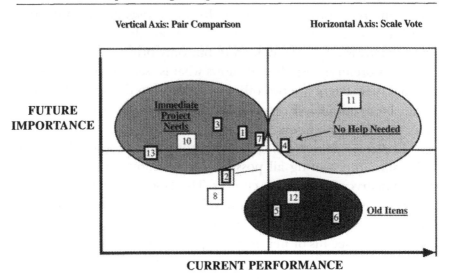

Exhibit 1.5   Sample Risk Filter Map

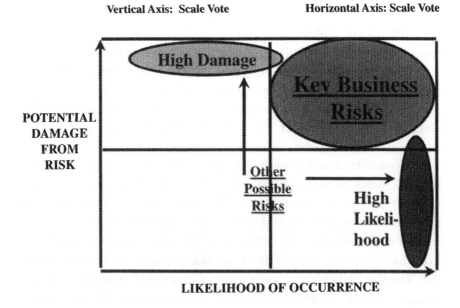

Exhibit 1.6   Sample Risk Control Map

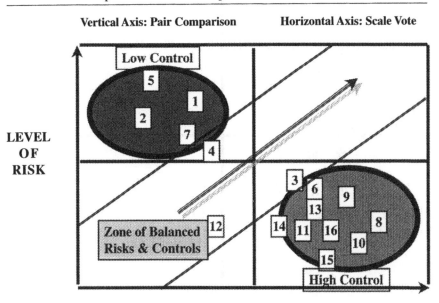

that no one's personal opinions are exposed to the group. When these are distributed, they provide immediate feedback on where there are significant differences between the group and an individual, and typically lead to fruitful discussions on those differences. Frequently these conversations help make progress in solving issues.

Finally, there is one last map output that is highly effective when shown to the participant group. This is called a scatter map and shows anonymously all individual votes that were averaged together to form the group maps discussed above. These scatters can show different patterns: tight agreement, loose agreement, confusion or disagreement, or polarization among subgroups. When seen by the participants, they reveal the "story behind the story"— whether a high-ranking priority is truly shared by all or whether there are significant differences within the group. Some of these scatter patterns are shown in Exhibits 1.7, 1.8 and 1.9.

Exhibit 1.7   Pattern of Agreement

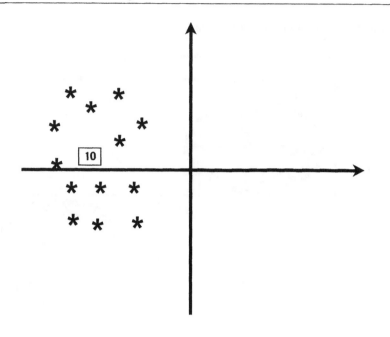

Exhibit 1.8   Disagreement or Confusion

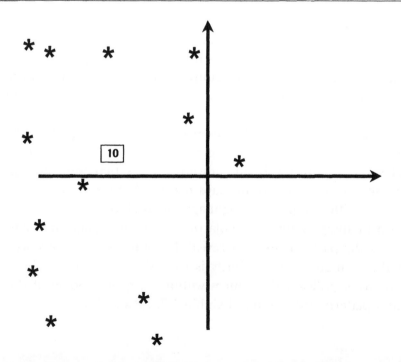

Exhibit 1.9   Pattern of Polarity

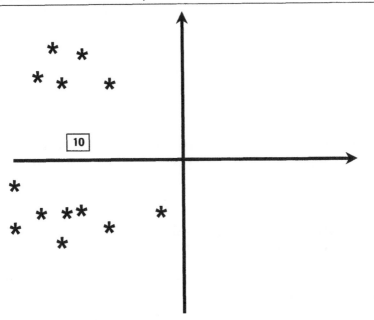

ROLE OF DIFFERENT CONTROL SELF-ASSESSMENT METHODOLOGIES

One of the most difficult issues with CSA is the custom creation of a CSA process that will obtain the specific results demanded by the client. This issue remains relatively unknown to most CSA consultants, who often develop a single process and use it for all varieties of problems. The critical importance of having the right CSA methodology, however, cannot be overemphasized. With the wrong CSA approach, the consulting engagement or audit plan will suffer in two major ways:

1. It will not have the full range of information needed by the client.
2. It will have wasted the client's time and energy by using an inappropriate approach.

Therefore, experienced facilitators should understand the need to design or modify their methodology as necessary to fit client needs. Certainly there are major CSA styles focused on common consulting needs, but even these need modification to fit specific situations. Also, the truly effective consultant occasionally will need to develop an entirely new approach to fit a unique problem.

Here at the beginning of the study of CSA, the methodology issue will be bypassed for the sake of simplicity. A single approach will be defined in later chapters and used as the core teaching example. The issue of designing special frameworks and methodologies to fit special needs will be examined in Chapter 8.

IMPORTANCE OF CONTROL SELF-ASSESSMENT AND FACILITATIVE CONSULTING

The advent of new, facilitative techniques for internal auditors and management consultants promises to be a major event in the growth of these professions. In the past, techniques often pitted auditors and consultants against their clients. Facilitation methodologies, however, help them become the consultative partners of their clients. Facilitation also helps obtain information that has both factual content and the perspectives and buy-in of various stakeholders. This perceptual information is critical in forging a workable, lasting solution to problems, and means that client organizations can put solutions into place that are better, faster, and less expensive.

In the usual course of events, determining the facts, the causation, and the solution of business problems is impossible within reasonable time limits. Usually only two can be determined at the expense of the third. But when an improved process is developed, then all three are possible. That is the role that facilitative consulting will play in the future, with CSA providing a methodology that enables organizations to get to the facts, the causation, and the solution of business problems at reasonable cost.

24

2

Understanding the Basis of Facilitation: Models to Remember

Many critics consider facilitation to be a "soft" technique—that is, one that has no real theory or basis, no underlying foundation that describes how it works. In the early days, that may have been true, as experimenters and researchers sought to find the best and most effective techniques. Today, however, a number of models explain the methodology. New facilitators must understand these models, which greatly speed up their learning curve.

TIME VERSUS PLACE MODEL

A basic "Where are we now?" model categorizes meetings according to time and place, as shown in Exhibit 2.1. For each time/place combination, the boxes also show which form of technology can be used to improve its effectiveness.

In this method of categorizing meetings, we separate "same time" from "different time." For example, a same-time meeting is the usual type that is attended by a workgroup to discuss business operations, solve problems, and so on. Typically such meetings are held in a single room, face to face, and are also labeled as same

Exhibit 2.1   The "Big Picture" of Meetings

CSA Is Here

Same Time / Same Place *Electronic* *Voting*	**Same Time / Different Place** *Video-/Teleconference*
Different Time / Same Place *War Rooms*	**Different Time / Different Place** *GroupWare* *(Lotus Notes®, etc.)*

place. So a *same-time/same-place* meeting is the one we are most familiar with.

Other types of meetings include different time/same place, same time/different place, and different time/different place.

Different Time/Same Place.   In many large businesses as well as in the military, there are advantages to having a single room set aside to assist in planning complex operations. These rooms are often called situation rooms, decision centers, or similar titles. The advantage of such locations is that various team members can come into this space, which is typically arranged with status reports of team progress, areas of difficulty, available resources, and so on. Here the environment is intended to help individuals or groups solving the given situation. And, as one group makes progress, it leaves its ideas in the room for others to study and improve upon.

Same Time/Different Place.   This type of meeting usually is conducted over electronic communications channels. It includes teleconferencing (telephone conference call between a number of different locations), videoconferencing (the same approach, but using both video and sound), and Internet conferencing (identical to videoconferencing, but using specialized Internet audio/video systems).

Different Time/Different Place. This is often called a virtual meeting and is one of the features available through Lotus Notes® or other groupware systems. In this type of meeting, there are no face-to-face discussions, no situation rooms, and no audio/video-conferencing. Here a discussion database is established for selected individuals (the team) to exchange thoughts and ideas on a given subject. Different databases address different topics and often have different member lists. Subjects might include an accounts payable process improvement study, manufacturing problems related to parts unavailability, selecting the right health-care provider for the employee benefits package, and so on. When a group member opens the database, all past comments and ideas are available, and the participant's task is to study these inputs and contribute comments or further ideas. Since no one ever truly "meets" in this setting, the phrase "virtual meeting" has been coined to describe it.

SELECTING THE RIGHT TYPE OF MEETING

The selection criteria between the above four meeting types are basic:

○ Participant availability
○ Cost of transportation
○ Technology availability
○ Goal(s) of the meeting

Participant Availability

This is the single, most difficult issue when trying to arrange same-time/same-place meetings. And the longer the meeting, the more difficult arranging participant availability becomes. Another factor that also can make this a difficult hurdle is that certain managerial participants often choose not to be available, because they doubt the effectiveness of the meeting and/or the technique to be used (e.g., facilitation), or because they want to avoid a situation where they are required to speak openly when they do not wish to do so. How to solve this problem? In many cases, the meeting has to be positioned as critical to the solution of an important business issue. In other cases, it will be helpful to have the highest-ranking manager concerned issue the invitation; sometimes even the chief executive officer (CEO) of the company should do so.

In a few, isolated cases, one should consider carefully whether the reluctant meeting participant will exert a negative force on the meeting if forced to attend. In one CSA meeting a few years ago, the head of one division of a pharmaceutical company was openly hostile to attending the scheduled facilitated meeting or to having his division managers attend. Whatever his reasons were, he simply refused to go until the company's CEO ordered him to attend. The meeting was scheduled to last four to six hours, with three hours of group discussion and intermittent electronic voting on different aspects of the business process. Once the meeting started, this division head was openly hostile and made statements to discourage his people from contributing. The facilitator, having no real discussion developing, conducted the first electronic vote but the division head ordered that there should be no discussion of its results. The outcome was that all electronic votes were conducted, one after the other, over a total of 30 minutes. The division head then stood, announced the meeting was over, and led his troops out of the room. Later that same division head complained to the CEO that the meeting was entirely useless and ineffectual, and should not be tried again.

One can sometimes spot personalities such as the man just described. They often "manage" through fear and intimidation, are open to no one's ideas but their own, disseminate little information under the information-is-power theory, and prevent their reports from operating as an entrusted team. This type of individual is poison to any facilitation session, and should be avoided at all costs.

Such "difficult" participants may be present in 1 percent of facilitation sessions, and in none at all if facilitators are sensitive to the psychology of the invited participants.

Often the easiest way to overcome objections is to meet with these individuals separately and describe the process to be used. The effectiveness of facilitated meetings should be emphasized, since they often solve in one to two days problems that have evaded solution for years. Why? Because all participants necessary to the solution are seated in the same room and each is hearing all of the others when they speak. Thus, as the discussion moves along, each comment is made with the awareness of others' comments, and suggestions are typically volunteered that incorporate others' ideas and preferences.

Finally, when people try to avoid the meeting simply because of unfamiliarity with the process, one can schedule the meeting so far in the future (e.g., 4 to 6 weeks) that participants' schedules are unlikely to be full.

Cost of Transportation

Having numerous participants travel to attend a meeting is costly to the business. As a result, new solutions are always under consideration. Travel manager–oriented magazines have recently shown the trade-off in cost, comparing physical travel to the use of video-conferenced meetings. In many cases, corporate travel managers are given management of the videoconferencing facility and asked to decrease travel costs through electronic conferencing. This is a new trend but one that is sure to grow.

Videoconferences, however, do not have the "look and feel" of a live, face-to-face meeting, an issue that must be factored in to the meeting planner's considerations. With two sites, the personal contact is decreased, but not significantly. One can place an oversize viewing screen at the end of each room's conference table. Participants in location A see the location B participants as if they are at the other end of the table, and vice versa. These devices increase the perceived reality of the meeting and help make it more effective. As the number of locations increase, however, the videoconferencing tool becomes more difficult to use in a group-participation mode. For making policy announcements, however, it can still be very effective and cost-saving.

Technology Availability

Since all but same-time/same-place meetings involve extra expense (videoconference system, situation room not used for general office space, etc.), many companies now can offer only real-time meetings. While this may seem less expensive in capital outlay, there is time wasted in arranging face-to-face meetings—time that often is critical when a problem has erupted and may damage the company. It also increases travel expense: airfare, hotel, meals, ground transportation. Therefore, it is recommended that meeting technology—videoconferencing, teleconferencing, discussion databases (Lotus Notes®, etc.) be considered.

Goal(s) of the Meeting

Some subjects require face-to-face interaction, and some do not. A group brainstorming session to solve a critical problem needs direct human interaction; however, an internal announcement of a new employee healthcare plan does not. The meeting planner has to choose which type of meeting is appropriate.

FACILITATION: A SAME-TIME/SAME-PLACE MEETING

Once that the advantages and disadvantages of each type of meeting have been highlighted, this book will focus on a single category: same-time/same-place meetings, led by a facilitator and organized to achieve a stated goal.

Why only same-time/same-place meetings? Because facilitated meetings depend on high levels of information transfer between participants, the type that occurs only when they are in a physical setting where each and every participant can hear all comments, respond at will, and thereby add to the group's total concepts and ideas. The solutions that the group develops come from no single person, but from everyone's contributions at the meeting. As a result, the meeting must be organized in a way that all participants are "up close and personal"—the same-time/same-place meeting.

Some studies have been done on having a facilitated meeting by use of teleconferencing, but the meeting's effectiveness decreases greatly with each additional site—perhaps by as much as 50 percent, in this author's experience.

There are many skills and techniques used in a face-to-face meeting, some of which will be highlighted further on in this book. Some include:

- Building a group dynamic
- The many uses of a U-shape table
- Facilitator interventions
- Focusing the group's attention
- Drawing out comments signaled by body language

CORE FACILITATION MODEL

Researchers have debated for years why and how facilitation is effective, with little practical explanation. As a full-time facilitator and consultant, however, I believe that a simple, core model explains some of the process's advantages—advantages illustrated in Exhibit 2.2.

Core of the Model: The Group

Notice that the triangle at the core in Exhibit 2.2 represents the group being facilitated. The fact that this can be any group—from shopfloor to executive suite—is a key advantage of the facilitative process. Groups can be convened in any company, at any level, across any number of different departments, to discuss any issue, making facilitation a truly universal process. Some examples include:

- Executive managers seeking to define business risks and controls
- Shopfloor employees meeting to discuss manufacturing problems

Exhibit 2.2   Core Model of the Facilitation Process

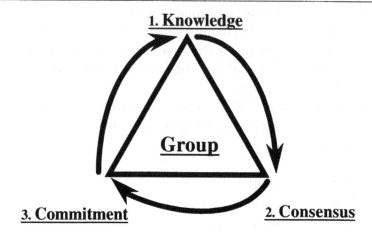

o Heads of different departments meeting to define their own information needs and the cross-communication feeds for a new computer system

o All department heads involved in an enterprisewide quality improvement initiative

One of the key features of facilitation is that it is a highly flexible tool. Nearly any group of individuals can use it to discuss and improve nearly any business issue. *The only consideration to keep in mind is that all participants must be either involved with the problem or potentially involved in the solution.* Extraneous personnel, observers, and those who oppose change should not participate. There is a place even for those trying to keep the status quo, however, since they will be able to voice appropriate objections to contemplated changes, perhaps speaking the thoughts of senior management. This may help better to define the solution plan or even suggest compromise solutions that will be achievable within that corporate culture.

Often it will be necessary to conduct an exercise to help blend a group of individuals into a focused group. One such technique is for the facilitator to first state the formal purpose of the meeting, and then ask each individual to state their name, department, and what his or her own individual purpose(s) might be in addition to the meeting's main purpose. At the end, the facilitator asks group members whether they understand and agree with the purpose of the meeting and whether it fits within their own individual goals. Usually participants respond by nodding, the signal that they now consider themselves to be working within a defined group.

Knowledge: The Top Corner of the Model

The knowledge component of the model represents all knowledge resident in the group. At the beginning of the meeting, this knowledge is individual and separated from others' knowledge. Through the meeting process, however, participants are asked to contribute their knowledge on a given subject. By the end of this contribution phase, the full group's knowledge has been "drained" from individuals, but a fully understood body of knowledge now has been formed by the group.

Gaining this knowledge through the contribution of individuals is the key first step of any solution process. Without that knowledge, and particularly without all members of the group sharing that knowledge, no breakthrough solutions can be gained.

One key concept to the sharing of knowledge is the understanding that often there are different perspectives on the facts of the situation—different perspectives held by different people, varying with each person's life experience, job responsibilities, and so on. When a member contributes these perspectives, all other participants are listening and integrating that perspective with their own. By the time the full group has contributed, all members have heard and absorbed the many different views held by the entire group. This greatly advances the discussion, since it often explains why different departments have behaved in varying, often conflicting ways when faced by the same situation. Sometimes, in fact, this stage of discussion will enable departments to understand how they have hindered each other in the past, and learn how to work together for greater efficiency and effectiveness.

Consensus: The Right Corner of the Model

Once the group's purpose and knowledge have been elicited, the next stage is to build a level of consensus within the meeting. Consensus in this case means sufficient agreement to move forward with the discussion, with an agreed problem, or with the final recommended solution.

A key point to remember is that consensus on major issues usually is built from consensus on numerous smaller issues. Not only is the meeting's objective agreed upon at the start (i.e., what is the key problem to be solved), but a group dynamic of working together to define issues and answers clearly also builds during the meeting. Thus, building small-issue consensus is a critical step leading to the later whole-problem/whole-solution consensus.

Another point to remember is that consensus tends to build by itself—it is not improved or accelerated by asking whether the group has gained consensus. It is essentially the by-product of a greater understanding that each participant has of the others' facts and perspectives. Therefore, the facilitator must increase that understanding by having speakers clarify their statements, asking follow-up questions, asking if the points made are clear to all group members, and generally treating all comments as food for further discussion. The eventual goal of consensus will be reached automatically, without artificial consensus-testing exercises, if the facilitator is patient and thoughtful in leading the discussion.

Thus, at the end of the knowledge discussion, a facilitator who has helped the group to gain understanding will not have to *develop* the group's consensus—it will be sufficient to find ways to *demonstrate* that that consensus already exists, as a natural result of the group contributions and discussion.

Commitment: The Left Corner of the Model

Assume that a meeting has been convened to solve a particular problem, such as minimizing scrap in a sheet-metal plant. Assume also that the group has successfully agreed to focus on the stated goals of the meeting, has contributed knowledge fully, and has reached consensus on the major components of the problems and some likely solutions.

At this point, the group must be led from the consensus stage to the commitment stage. This means going from a passive agreement ("Yes, these are the issues"), to an active willingness to participate in the solution ("I'll take on the shopfloor implementation role"). Attaining commitment is not automatic, but it is not difficult either. Commitment develops naturally as an outcome of the group's consensus on an issue. The key rule is that a plan developed through the full interaction of a group of people becomes "their plan." They are committed to its success because of their participation in creating it. That commitment soon becomes a willingness to participate in the rollout of the plan, establishing a core group of supporters that will ensure the plan's success.

FACILITATION PROCESS RELATED TO MEETING STAGES

To explain further how to advance the meeting, let us define the *activities* that are used to proceed to each of the *stages.* These are shown in the second model in Exhibit 2.3.

Gaining Understanding

Here we start to see the beginnings of the facilitative process—that is, how we get the meeting participants from one stage to another. For example, to move from Stage 1 (knowledge) to Stage 2 (consensus) will require a process to gain the group's understanding. This is a fairly simple process where the facilitator asks each participant for additional information and continually checks to make sure that all group members understand the contribution made, and its application to the problem area under discussion.

After contributions by numerous individuals, each of them facilitated to encourage discussion and improve understanding, the

Exhibit 2.3   Activity Model of the Facilitation Process

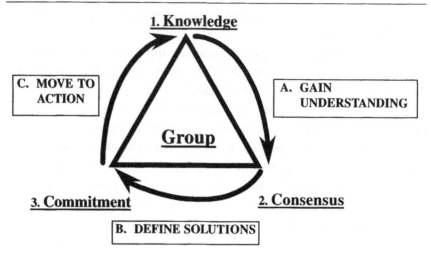

meeting will arrive at some sort of consensus. This may be only knowledge consensus where everyone agrees on the body of knowledge accumulated, it may move forward to defining likely areas where solutions might be found, or it may automatically move into the next process, defining solutions. All this is enabled simply through the process of helping the group gain understanding of the knowledge contributed by all members.

Defining Solutions—A Practical Method

Assuming that the group has achieved a mutual understanding of each other's knowledge and perspectives, now is the time to start shaping that understanding into a useful outcome, a solution to the problem under discussion. Frequently the information gathered will point to some obvious solution steps. The facilitator's role in this case is simply to ask the question "What do these facts suggest?" This will start participants down the solution track. In other cases, the solutions may not be so obvious. Here, additional creativity is needed, and the facilitator must establish an open, creative atmosphere within the group. Numerous creativity exercises and methods exist, many of which are documented at length in meeting planning books. From the author's experience, however, one technique has proven most effective: *Post-it Notes with affinity grouping.* The technique works as follows:

1. Establish the key question to be answered. For example, "How to increase production quality and still lower costs?"

2. Ensure that all group members understand the meaning of the question.

3. Inform the group, through words or creativity exercises, that this is an opportunity to think "out of the box." Past attempts to solve these conflicting parameters (high production quality versus low cost) using typical thought processes have failed, so it is up to group members to go beyond the usual limits in answering the question.

4. Have a silent "creativity period" of 20 to 30 minutes, during which all group members jot down as many creative ideas and solutions that they can think of. Each idea should be brief—no details—and the measure of success should be a large number of ideas from all participants. Even ideas that seem illogical should be recorded, since they may turn out to be implementable when combined with the ideas of other participants.

5. At the end of the idea-recording stage, ask the group to give you one single idea on a Post-it Note. Perhaps the note would say "Organize into work teams, not assembly lines." The facilitator's question would then be "What category would this idea fit into?" One possible answer might be "Restructuring work methods."

6. Then go to a wall on which numerous blank flipchart sheets have been mounted (perhaps 15 to 20 sheets along the wall). The Post-it Note is mounted on the first sheet as the first idea and the title of the sheet—Restructuring Work Methods—is written at the top in bold letters.

7. Ask participants to present all ideas that relate to restructuring work methods. All these ideas are mounted in a random fashion on that flipchart sheet.

8. Then ask for a new idea, one that has nothing to do with restructuring work methods. A new idea is volunteered, and steps 5 to 8 of this exercise are repeated.

9. Continue this exercise until all major categories of ideas are exhausted and nearly all idea notes have been mounted. (The remaining few go on a sheet labeled "Other.")

10. Then invite participants to choose a subject shown on one sheet and to organize the ideas into some rational order. If more than one person works on a sheet/category, even better; the group will benefit from their joint thoughts on the ideas. This is done for all sheets.

11. After all sheets have been organized, ask each person/group responsible for a sheet to report to the entire group on the ideas presented, the patterns formed by those ideas, and possible undercurrents of other ideas that have been detected.

12. After all sheet presentations are complete, have the full group discuss major ideas that have come out of the exercise, their implementability, and their relationship to other ideas. Then all topics should be voted—electronically or manually—to determine key strategies.

Moving to Action

Once there is consensus and some early-stage ideas and solutions, the group will start to move toward the commitment stage of the process. Again, this happens almost automatically and depends greatly on the content that has been developing through the facilitative process. It also requires that the facilitator act as a helper, not as a "pusher," and certainly not as a participant. Once the facilitator moves into a participant role, suggesting his or her own ideas, the group loses trust in the leader's neutrality. Similarly, the facilitator should not push the group too hard; doing so will earn their hostility.

The group is now at a delicate point: There are many ideas, some of them traditional and some quite new. The task now is to move these ideas into a workable action plan, harnessing the commitment that the group has built up by working together.

13. Assign each highly voted strategy to a subgroup, have it investigate all aspects of its ideas, and then report to the main group on its results. Usually subgroups are organized according to those sheets that have the most promise to bringing about the desired solution. Each subgroup is given a number of Planning Form Sheets, such as the one shown in Exhibit 2.4, to standardize the reporting format and to ensure that all aspects of the proposed plan are addressed.

14. Inform each subgroup that the top line must refer to the category it has been investigating (Restructuring Work

Exhibit 2.4   Planning Form for Solution Strategies

Key Strategy: *Restructuring Work Methods*

Description of Tactic:

Organize into work teams, not assembly lines

Person(s) Responsible:

Special Resources or Skills Required?

Person-weeks: *2-4*   Investment Required: $ *15,000*

Special Skills:

Outsourceable?   Yes:_____   No: *✓*   Comments: *internal pilot share*

Action Steps and Milestones:

   1. Involve Human Resources department

   2. Gain shopfloor support

   3. Conduct series of pilot tests

Performance Measures:

   (1) Length of retraining, (2) Quality of manufactured output, (3) Time to manufacture, (4) Innovative ideas

---

Methods, Capital Equipment Investment, Work Incentives, etc.). Then, below that, the group reporters describe specific ideas that have been developed in the subgroup discussions. Each idea should be briefly stated, taking up only one page, and should include as much planning data as possible.

15. After all subgroups have reported to the full meeting and after all major ideas have been presented, have the full group vote their preferences among the individual action plans; that is, they vote their preference for each idea represented on a Planning Form sheet. (Scale vote—1 to 9, for example.)

16. The final results of the voting will show a ranked list of ideas and solution strategies, every one formed through group discussion and individual involvement. This is an effective beginning to a formal action plan, which is the next step for the group to accomplish before adjourning. The action plan will be more than just a collection of ideas—it will include numerous perspectives, final smoothing of interdepartmental issues, and probably budgets to implement the plan.

The process just described works well in nearly any group seeking an action plan. Note, however, that action planning is different from Control Self-Assessment. Planning meetings always are concerned with the future: future solutions, future corporate strategies, future budget development, and so on. When the word "planning" is used, the process listed above is highly useful.

One element just mentioned is the voting of participants' preferences. Although there are a number of manual methods for doing this, I recommend that organizations invest in an electronic voting system. These systems enable participants to vote anonymously, to have their voting displayed immediately after voting, and to have the voting data organized in different ways to see the levels of consensus, the areas of recommended investment, areas where money can be saved, and the like.

STAGES OF FACILITATION EXPERTISE

Many companies consider facilitators to be merely meeting moderators who help keep participants on focus. There are, however, higher objectives that can be achieved, including leading a group to better results than it could achieve individually. Reaching that higher result is the purpose of this book, and (to attain those levels one must understand the stages of facilitation expertise:)

- Values conversion
- Meeting leadership
- Consulting focus
- Specific methodologies

Level I: Values Conversion

Facilitation involves different beliefs and different values from traditional consulting. Here the meeting leader is not acting as an expert in the subject matter under discussion. Rather, the facilitator is a "process expert" helping clients share information and develop solutions. To be effective, facilitators must drop the usual "content expert" role. In fact, a facilitator who tries to inform or assist the participants in developing any particular solution can seriously hinder progress in a meeting.

Tied into the process expert role is the understanding that the clients or participants have all the knowledge needed to come up with the necessary answers or solutions. Although this may seem to be an overstatement, it is true. In my experience, where content experts have been present to supply additional input, I have never seen that input add significantly to the results of the meeting. The participants have always had the necessary working knowledge and experience to bring new ideas and insights to a problem, once the meeting developed into an open discussion and idea-generating session.

As a beginning facilitator, it will be helpful to participate in meetings and practice helping others contribute their ideas and solutions. The more that one encourages others to participate, the more other participants will appreciate one's presence and contribution to the meeting. Facilitators—no longer acting as participants—may change their emphasis from "I know the answer" to "What do we all know that might help?"

As simple as this sounds, it is the single most difficult attitude change for traditional consultants to adopt. Most content-expert consultants have difficulty dropping their knowledge and expertise when leading a facilitation session. And, in every case, their leadership value weakens considerably when they fall back into suggesting ideas that come from their own expertise.

Even when the group is stalled on an issue, even when its information seems insufficient, a facilitator cannot drop into the content-expert role. Not only will the information be rejected (because it comes from an "outsider"), it usually will be far less helpful than ideas coming from those involved with the problem on a day-to-day basis.

In summary, these are the basic values to learn:

- Being facilitative: Asking, not telling; gaining agreement from the group
- Understanding the importance of group input
- Learning that patience brings far better results
- Learning that nearly all information can be valuable
- Seeing patterns of discussion and behavior

Once these values have been understood, practiced, and ingrained, it is time to move on to facilitative meeting leadership.

Level II: Meeting Leadership

For a facilitator, there are 15 key steps to understand—before, during, and after the meeting. These are shown in Exhibit 2.5, and described in detail in Appendix A.

Any beginning facilitator must understand that there is a structure and a science (even if it is a "soft" one) in running an effective, facilitated meeting. The organizational guide in Appendix A is equally useful in conducting CSA meetings, strategic planning sessions, and other meetings.

Exhibit 2.5   Facilitation Guide

I. Preparation	II. Conduct	III. Reporting and Follow-Up
1. Understand and Identify Issues	1. Facilitator is Fully Skilled in the Process	1. Write Participants' Report
2. Establish Clear Objectives for Session	2. Use Correct Facilitation Technology	2. Write Client's Report
3. Determine Methodology for Session	3. Understand Depth and Specificity Required	3. Ensure Action Items Are Completed
4. Prepare for Session	4. Develop Group Consensus and Commitment	4. Establish Plans for Longer-Term Items
5. Schedule Time, Invite Participants	5. Create Record of Words and Voting Data	5. Review Engagement; Seek Additional Needs

Even without extensive detail, however, it is clear that leading a meeting is not a casual effort. Facilitators must be prepared, must understand their appropriate role, and must lead the group to its stated objective without being a content contributor.

Some of the learning objectives at this stage include:

○ Group dynamics
  ○ When to push versus when to pull
  ○ When interventions are needed
  ○ Whether objectives are being achieved
○ Other objectives defined by the client
○ Keeping to the agenda in both subject matter and time
○ Keeping participants involved

To learn, it would be helpful to take a course in facilitation technique. However, even without such a course, anyone can practice by offering to help lead meetings in their company or organization—specifically, meetings where they would not be chosen as a content contributor. Facilitators should "start small," build experience, and slowly expand their skills into more complex meetings and larger audiences. (Facilitation is ideally conducted in a group of 10 to 20 people. Larger groups become much more difficult to manage, given the exponential growth in the number of interpersonal relationships occurring. Smaller groups are difficult because of the lack of broad information.)

Level III: Consulting Focus

The next stage in facilitator expertise is to adopt a consultant's perspective in leading the meeting. Once practiced in general meeting leadership and in helping participants to focus and develop consensus, a facilitator needs to understand how to focus a group on a stated objective or purpose. An agenda is helpful but is not an objective. It merely sets forth the steps to get to that objective. What types of objectives qualify?

- ○ Control self-assessment
- ○ Strategic planning
- ○ Marketing planning
- ○ Budget planning
- ○ Business risk analysis
- ○ Significant problem analysis/resolution

Each of these meetings has a different objective and therefore a different methodology or agenda. What is hidden behind these objectives, however, is even more important. Some are focused on potential future events (planning), and some are focused on discovering or solving existing situations (control self-assessment, business risk analysis, and problem analysis/resolution). These are the two major categories of facilitation.

Specific learning objectives for this stage of expertise include the following:

- ○ Understanding client needs
- ○ Formulating an agenda to meet those needs
- ○ Leading the group in a *focused* discussion
- ○ Eliciting specific information needed to achieve client goals

44

As this book is focused on CSA, none of the future-oriented planning objectives are described. However, there are numerous courses in these techniques, often called creativity meetings. The central focus here is the analysis of risks and controls, or of business processes or problems, using the CSA technique developed in the late 1980s and since expanded by numerous consultants and consulting firms.

Level IV: Specific Methodologies

Even within a specific technique such as CSA, numerous methodologies can be used. The most accomplished facilitators can conduct CSA meetings in many different ways. This is because no single CSA methodology is appropriate to all situations, and, even within a given methodology, it is highly recommended to adapt the process to a particular client's needs.

For example, one client meeting may wish to examine the audit controls of a department in close detail and to redesign those that are found insufficient. Here, a methodology that examines the departmental controls in detail, one by one, would be most appropriate. But when a group of corporate executives wishes to examine all the business risks facing the organization, both internal and external, then a technique using a higher-level business risk model is preferred. Each of these methodologies is well suited for its particular purpose, but only experience will enable a facilitator to select the right methodology, given the client's needs, and to modify that methodology as needed.

The highest level of facilitation skill is the ability to create the right meeting methodology, the one that is best suited to achieve the needs of the client department or organization. It will come after years of experience but will also create a high demand for a facilitator's services. It is worth the effort.

Some of the rewards of this level of expertise include:

o Each methodology defines new areas of consulting business and revenue.
o Each methodology develops a separate area of expertise for servicing client needs.

- ○ Each drives new and different services to market.
- ○ Once a specific methodology is adopted, all consultants within a firm can obtain uniform results.
- ○ Each methodology can be applied to numerous new situations with minor customization.

Although these goals may seem impossibly distant for the beginning CSA facilitator, insights will grow with experience. When those insights become an ability to see the process problem and facilitation methodology problem together, many consultants will develop new CSA processes. We look forward to the day when CSA becomes a flexible and universal consulting tool.

3

Definitions and Distinctions

DISTINGUISHING CHARACTERISTICS

A number of different facilitation methods have developed over the past decades, each with its own techniques. Such methods include:

- Encounter groups
- Focus groups
- Team-building meetings
- Brainstorming/creativity meetings
- Total quality management (TQM) programs
- Facilitated planning meetings
- Control self-assessment meetings

Clearly, each style of meeting has its own purpose and specific methodologies to achieve that purpose. Some are future-focused, some are outcome-focused, some are focused on the perceptions and feelings of participants. How, then, can we define CSA, the most recent of these techniques? Here are seven characteristics of CSA that distinguish it from other methodologies:

1. It is focused on problems and their solutions.
   - In the internal audit field, these are phrased as "audit risks and controls" (the origin of the word "control" in the CSA name).

- In the general business consulting field, CSA is used most often for determining business risks and their controls or solutions.
- In the area of business process improvement, the focus is on inefficiencies, gaps, areas of miscommunication or noncooperation, and the like.

2. CSA is strictly present-oriented—it does not search for long-term future solutions or for creative strategies to change the direction of a company. It does, however, seek immediate solutions to existing problems.

3. CSA is a real-time interview of business clients, seeking to determine where there are problems and what solutions might be available.

4. Due to the group discussion format, using a trained facilitator, the added value of CSA over individual interviews is the sharing of all participants' perspectives on the questions at hand.

5. Most CSA sessions will move naturally from problem discussions to analyzing the root causes of those problems.

6. In a fully equipped CSA session, computers are used to transcribe participants' comments during the discussion, in a real-time mode. Electronic voting systems also are used to gather data on individual preferences and perceptions anonymously. These data are displayed visually on projection screens, where they help the group to understand

- their agreed priorities for allocating resources
- the greatest business risks, of those mentioned
- where the group agrees most on a solution, and where it is divided
- where a group's disagreement might align with participants' age, business departments, corporate location, or time in service ("demographic analysis")

7. CSA always is based on a framework—a description of the business process, a list of questions, a business risk model,

and so on. Sometimes this framework is explicit and openly used, and sometimes it is implicit. But without a framework, the CSA technique is not nearly as effective.

In addition to these characteristics, there are two clear benefits of CSA that need to be mentioned:

1. When a group is engaged in discussion of business issues or analyzing a business process or problem, CSA will nearly always reveal the "holes" in the organization or process that have not been handled properly. These could take the form of organizational gaps, poor handoffs between departments, or areas that have simply not been included in the planning of a strategy. This is unique to CSA, and is a major consulting advantage.
2. The participants in a CSA session will share ownership of the solutions developed in that session, as occurs in nearly all facilitated meeting techniques. Anyone not included in the meeting will not share in that ownership and will be difficult to bring to the same level of commitment. Therefore, any facilitated meeting that will develop action plans always should include the full array of people needed for implementation.

Each of these distinctions and benefits is examined in more detail below.

FOCUS ON PROBLEMS AND THEIR SOLUTIONS

Using a military metaphor, both logn-range and short-range artillery are needed in battle. CSA is clearly a short-range tool, in the sense that it can focus tightly on a single problem, bring individuals into a meeting that understanding the problem, and come up with immediate answers to the situation.

This is not to say that CSA cannot be used for large problems or for long-term issues; but its clear distinction is the ability to focus narrowly and get immediate answers. Once the meeting's purpose moves toward developing major new policies and directions involving creative problem-solving techniques, we have gone beyond CSA's central capabilities.

What types of problems can CSA handle? Nearly anything that can be discussed in a business setting. This author has facilitated sessions as widely diverse as:

- Analyzing business risks across a major insurance company, with all vice presidents and the CEO in attendance
- Reviewing the engine breakdown and rebuilding process in a heavy-equipment remanufacturing plant, interviewing shopfloor and supervisory personnel
- Analyzing product deficiencies in a pharmaceutical setting
- Finding new ways to analyze fraud risk for a major national bank

In all these sessions, CSA was used to focus on the given problem and to develop needed solutions. (In the "Framework" discussion that follows and in subsequent chapters, we examine how a single technique can have such a broad diversity of focus.)

PRESENT-TENSE ORIENTATION

The major difference between the CSA process and previous strategic planning techniques is its focus on the "here and now." In its simplest description, CSA is nothing more than an interview on a specific business problem, but performed in a group setting.

One of the reasons that the present-tense orientation is so important is that the focus on current problems had not been a major facilitation focus before CSA. Nearly all facilitative consulting techniques involved some type of plan—a new strategic plan, marketing plan, or budget plan—all future-oriented; or a new approach to quality, sometimes requiring new processes/reorganizations.

Focus groups were developed to understand participants' current perceptions of advertisements or products, but they were not used to solve the problems. Rather, the perceptions gathered in the focus group were taken back to the "professionals" to fix.

So CSA is the first facilitation technique that not only interviews participants on problems but also asks them to suggest solutions. Here the group is truly in the present tense. There is a situation that needs fixing, and they are the ones selected to fix it. They are also, by their selection, the right group to come up with answers.

These factors add together to make a CSA meeting an intense environment, where participants stay tightly focused on the present. If they stray, the facilitator must bring them back into that problem-solving focus.

REAL-TIME INTERVIEW OF CLIENTS

If there is any simple way to plan a CSA session, it is to envision an interview with a single client on the given subject matter. Scripting questions for that interview often can serve as the beginning of an agenda for interviewing 10 to 20 clients at the same time. Yes, the session is more formal; yes, the structure of the meeting is more intentional. But the group interview will, in many ways, follow the same sequence as that of an individual, in-depth interview. The major difference, and the major source of CSA's added value, is the sharing of perspectives among participants.

SHARING OF PERSPECTIVES

When a single business client is interviewed, data are recorded by the interviewer for later analysis. After all interviews are complete, the team of interviewers gathers together to compare answers and develop insights as to the underlying issues. Then they formulate a report to the clients, highlighting those issues and suggesting solutions.

The weakness of this approach is that both the insights and the solutions are developed by outsiders, professional consultants who do not work in the problem situation on a daily basis. Therefore, the insights and solutions do not have the benefit of client input until they are formally presented. This is why most consulting plans, when first presented, need major rework to be effective in the client environment.

When the clients are involved in a group interview, however, the situation has changed significantly. If Manager A, for example, describes a problem relating to lack of appropriate parts inventory, there will probably be a reaction from Manager B, who is responsible for maintaining that inventory. This may expand to a discussion with the chief financial officer regarding the insufficiency of capital allocation to parts inventories. In other words, the problem is fully exposed and fully discussed.

The key to this perspective-sharing is that, when one client is speaking, the others are listening. And, when listening, they will absorb the new information that has been given—not just the facts of the situation but the perspective of the speaker. By the time all factual answers have been contributed, meeting participants understand a full range of data as well as the business perspectives of their coparticipants. Often the root causes of the problem become clear. For example:

- Assembly Line Manager: "The parts we are getting are dirty, and we waste our time cleaning them prior to assembly."
- Inventory Manager: "We have been told to stock all parts in their original cartons, still packed in grease and sealed, to prevent loss and improve tracking of stock."
- Suggestion from other manager: "Why not have a cleaning station set up between your departments, to handle parts on their way to assembly?"

Although this conversation may seem simple, it actually reflects many real discussions and real solutions developed during CSA sessions. Often suggestions come from managers not involved in the problem, since they have an unbiased and open view of the situation. Many suggestions may at first be unrealistic, but as the discussion continues the suggestions become more focused. Often, by the end of the discussion, a workable solution has been developed.

On more complex issues, the answers require more time and more formal effort to solve. But the sequence is the same: Those involved with the problem contribute their facts and views, and the entire meeting then pitches in to suggest potential solutions. This is a powerful tool that has helped to solve many issues that were previously considered insoluble.

ANALYZING THE ROOT CAUSES OF PROBLEMS

Discussions of problems often move to discussions of the causes of those problems. If not, it is a simple matter for the facilitator to ask why the problems occur, and what factors are common across the full set of problems under discussion. This moves the participants into an analytical discussion where causation is the focus. Questions focus on why the problems arise, where they first occur, what dynamics have kept them occurring, and what assumptions need to be questioned in the organization or business process.

This causation discussion among participants is an efficient way to get to the right answers. When answers are produced by outside consultants, the background information is usually incomplete or very expensive to develop. But the working participants know far more than they realize about the problem situation. They know their organization, their work experience, the ways people interact in the workplace, and so on. So a causation discussion often gets to the underlying root causes in a minimum of time when using CSA techniques.

COMPUTER-BASED SYSTEMS FOR VOTING
AND TRANSCRIPTION

The use of computers during a CSA session is optional but highly valuable. There are two types of systems, each with its own valuable contribution to the session.

Transcription Systems

A transcription system is nothing more complex than projecting the computer screen image while transcribing comments using word processing software. The comments can be transcribed verbatim as a running record of the session, but this requires highly skilled typists. Another option is to prepare a template of specific questions before the session and enter participants' answers into the template during the discussion. Since the screen image is projected for all participants, they can make corrections during the conversation as well as review others' comments for deeper insight. By the end of the session, a validated record has been built that will memorialize the comments and the insights of the session.

The use of computerized transcription systems adds significantly to the value of the meeting. From a recording perspective, there is a permanent record of the session. More important, however, is the analytical value of the record: In a large engagement involving numerous CSA meetings (different management groups, different locations, different employee levels, etc.), the same questions are asked in all sessions. Having a written record, question by question, gives the consultant a cross-comparison capability that is far better than informal note-taking.

Electronic Voting Systems

Electronic voting systems (described in Chapter 10) enable participants to vote anonymously on various questions posed by the facilitator. Not only can a single question ("How efficient is this process?") be answered in a quantitative way, but two- and three-dimensional displays can be constructed, combining data from different questions. Exhibits 3.1 and 3.2 illustrate two examples of CSA voting results.

Electronic voting adds value that cannot be obtained reasonably in any other way, even with hand-voting techniques. Electronic voting allows rapid, in-depth analysis of participants' preferences and priorities in a real-time display, right in front of the participant group. The voting provides the facilitator with significant material to ask questions that can open up the discussion:

○ Why certain choices are preferred

Exhibit 3.1　One-Dimensional Voting Survey

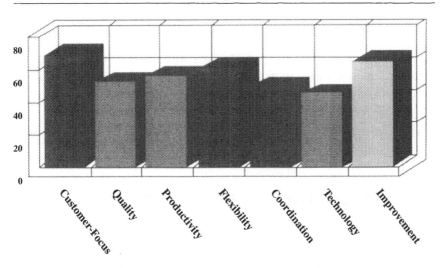

Exhibit 3.2　Two-Dimensional Voting Survey

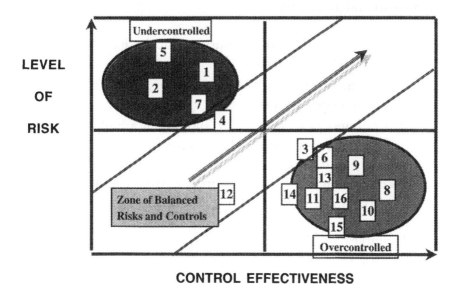

o Why there is so little consensus on choice A yet such high agreement on choice B
o What trends are shown in the voting data
o What investment strategies are suggested by the voting

Computerized voting quantifies and memorializes the perceptions of the participant group. It also provides a factual basis for recommending various solutions and investments to management. Management frequently supports recommendations made with voting data, particularly where there is high agreement among voters.

USE OF PROBLEM OR SOLUTION FRAMEWORK

Whether explicit or implicit, all CSA sessions are based on some sort of framework. At the most basic level, this framework could be a core set of questions that are asked. In multi-session CSA engagements, the same questions are asked and then answers compared across participant groups.

Frameworks, however, can be more complex and important to the session's outcome than a simple list of questions. Other types of frameworks might include:

o A business risk model, ensuring that the meeting discusses all possible types of risk.
o A research framework of issues under inquiry, where a contract has been granted.
o A business process diagram, showing at a high level all the components of a successful business process as a guide to participants' examination of problem areas. The diagram could include any business process, from manufacturing, to marketing, to financial.

Examples of these types of frameworks are displayed in Exhibits 3.3, 3.4, and 3.5.

Exhibit 3.3   Example of a Business Risk Model

Financial Operations	**Product Operations**	**Employee**
Credit Availability	Product Quality	Commitment
Interest Rates	Business Interruption	Efficiency
		Honesty

Information Risk		
Product Information	Business Information	Market Information

External Risk		
Legal	Capital Markets	Acts of God
Economic	Competition	Regulation

Exhibit 3.4   Example of a Research Framework

I I.   I M P L E M E N T A T I O N   I S S U E S

Implications of CSA Adoption for IA, Management, and Directors	Steps to Accelerate CSA Implementation and Added Value

Implications of CSA for Internal Audit	Implications of CSA for Management	Principal Lessons Learned by Mature Users	Ability to Transfer Lessons Learned
Implications of CSA for Directors	Nature of Change Process Implicated	Ability to Replicate Elements of Success	Which Strategies to Employ

Exhibit 3.5   Engine Remanufacture Process Framework

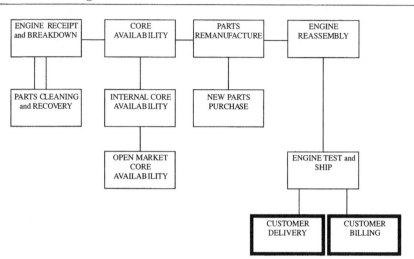

REVEALING THE HOLES IN THE ORGANIZATION OR PROCESS

A number of business texts have referred to the "white spaces" in an organization, "silo thinking," and "stovepipe mentalities." All these phrases refer to organizations that have a definite structure, but either the structure has left significant gaps, or the workers do not think outside their departmental boundaries.

In a CSA discussion focused on a particular problem, the presence of a broad group of participants ensures that gaps and poor communication are prevented, at least for the duration of that meeting. For example, if the discussion is focused on improving the accounts payable (A/P) process, it would be natural to include heads of departments that are affected negatively by poor A/P response.

In one such CSA session led by the author, it was found that 28 percent of the A/P department's time was taken up by auditing only 5 percent of the cash flowthrough—that is, auditing and approving employee expense reports. Since the meeting included the entire

A/P department, the cause was quickly spotted; it was due to the failure of employees' managers to disapprove improper expenses. The situation was caused by personal discomfort on the part of managers who dealt with the employees on a day-to-day basis. They all knew that "someone" would check the expense reports before checks were issued. In this case, the audit controls flowed downstream to the A/P department, where clerks had to review and audit nearly every expense report in the company.

The solution? Once the cause was found, the solution was simple: "Just say no!" With the agreement of the other departmental managers at the meeting, the A/P department stopped auditing all but a few sample expense reports. Employees stopped receiving their checks in a timely fashion, and their supervising managers were forced to start exercising their appropriate control responsibilities. The result? A 23 percent savings in A/P resources, practically overnight.

This example shows where a gap in audit controls can be highlighted and resolved easily. Many other gaps exist in today's complex business organizations. Typically, however, they are difficult to find. When a CSA meeting is focused on a particular business issue, it is nearly certain to spot those organizational gaps and miscommunications that directly relate to that problem.

SHARING OWNERSHIP OF SOLUTIONS DEVELOPED

In one sense, CSA is like many other facilitated techniques. Once a group of clients has participated in building a solution together, the individuals from that meeting have a sense of ownership of that solution. Thereafter, they are willing supporters and participants in the implementation of the fix.

This is an almost automatic result of groups involved in discussion and development of plans, problem resolutions, and process improvements. In the long run, it may the single greatest advantage of using the facilitative process in helping your organization to succeed.

4

A Control Self-Assessment Session to Improve Business Performance

VIEWING BUSINESS AS A SET OF PROCESSES

The single most important—and sometimes most difficult—step in improving business performance is to view the entire organization as a set of processes. Initially this may seem little different from reviewing the various departments in the organization, but it soon leads down different paths.

Take, for example, the accounts payable (A/P) function: Certainly it is served by an A/P department, but the personnel of that department do not represent the whole process, nor do they perform all necessary steps for the process to be effective. Consider the other necessary participants in the A/P process:

- Vendors, who supply goods and generate invoices
- The receiving department, which checks out that the invoices match the goods sent
- Quality control (or similar function), which verifies that the goods are supplied as specified and operate correctly

- The organization's customers, whose purchases supply the necessary funds for operating the enterprise
- The finance department, which allocates sufficient funds for invoices payment
- The organization's banking services supplier, which ensures the availability of those funds through checking account transactions, electronic funds transfers, and the like
- The National Clearing House, which ensures the free flow of funds between banks and their clients

For an accounts payable department to be successful, all these inputs need to operate successfully. A/P personnel perform the central transactions that bring these various participants into concerted action, but they are not the entire process in themselves.

The same is true for all other departments and operations in a functioning enterprise. Each process has its own inputs and outputs and performs its own specific function, to ensure that the entire process is performed correctly and efficiently.

STRUCTURE OF BUSINESS PROCESSES

Every business process, therefore, has its own unique structure. At the highest and simplest level, these can be classified as:

- Input (or Cause)
- Operation (or Event)
- Output (or Effect)

Exhibit 4.1 shows how this structure might be depicted.

For a single business process, the structure seems relatively straightforward. When one considers an entire enterprise, however, there are thousands of combinations of business processes working alongside, and sometimes overlaying, each other. Consider, for example, the engine rebuilding example from the last chapter, depicted in Exhibit 4.2.

Exhibit 4.1   Business Process Events

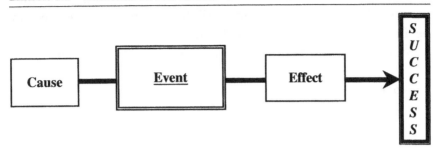

Hardly any of the subprocesses in Exhibit 4.2 can operate alone. Therefore, to analyze the entire manufacturing process, it is necessary to examine each of its component parts and their interactions.

BUSINESS PROCESS ANALYSIS: SELECTING THE PURPOSE

The examination of the component parts of a process (the sub-processes) is not a simple matter, because first one has to identify *the*

Exhibit 4.2   Engine Remanufacture Process Framework

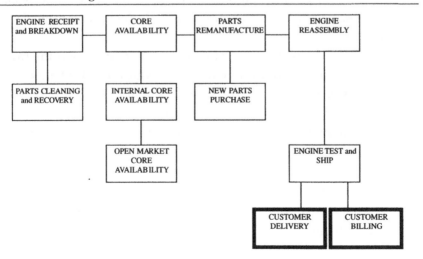

purpose of the examination. Without a clear understanding of that purpose, the business process analysis will be off target. The results may be fully accurate but will not be useful to achieve the desired improvement. Sample process improvement purposes include:

- ○ Efficiency
- ○ Quality
- ○ Capital expense
- ○ Business risk
- ○ Potential time savings

With any form of business process analysis, one has to match the research to the desired purpose. Many forms of process analysis are suited to only a single purpose, such as quantitative techniques seeking to improve efficiency. One unique aspect of Control Self-Assessment, however, is that it can be used for *any inquiry, regarding any business process, in any business enterprise.*

This may seem to be an overstatement. However, the true test is "What are the limits of human conversation?" Since Control Self-Assessment is a structured form of interpersonal discussion, its limits are as broad as those of conversation itself. Naturally, this won't extend to quantitative measures that can be achieved only through mechanical devices (e.g., high-temperature sensors), but the *results* and the *meaning* of those measurements is a legitimate topic for a CSA session.

Looking at the engine remanufacturing process framework again, we could research many different issues in a CSA meeting. The difference would be the questions asked and the particular sub-processes on which we focus our attention.

For example, if our study were to improve process efficiency, we might ask the following questions:

- ○ How much does each step of the process cost?
- ○ What contribution does this make to the final product price?
- ○ Which steps occupy the most, and the least, labor to complete?

Again focusing on process efficiency, it is likely that our attention would be drawn more to the labor-intensive subprocesses as shown in Exhibit 4.3.

Different subprocesses would receive high attention in different situations. Safety factors would focus on manual labor steps, while cost savings might look at the cost of purchasing new parts from outside vendors versus recovering used ones from older engines.

CHOOSING THE RIGHT PERSPECTIVE

In addition to selecting the right purpose for the inquiry, it is also important to understand the organizational perspective that is being used. There are three key choices:

1. *Horizontal:* A lateral discussion, involving representatives of different departments, typically employees at a similar managerial level
2. *Vertical:* A departmental discussion, involving a top-to-bottom cross-section of a department—perhaps the entire process
3. *Diagonal:* A discussion with representatives from across the organization, chosen for their involvement with a specific process

Exhibit 4.3 Efficiency-Related Processes

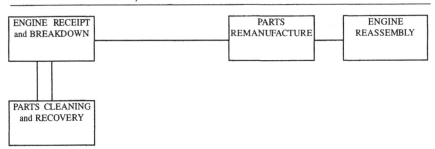

Horizontal examinations are broad by nature. Often they involve a large representation of managers, drawn together for some kind of "company review." Most frequently, these sessions are at a vice-presidential to CEO level, and may focus on examining business risks. They could just as well be engineering reviews or sales reviews. One of the key features of this type of meeting is that it rarely involves more than two contiguous levels of management, and at most three levels. This is due to the breadth of the discussion and the need for all participants to be able to look at the business situation from the same "altitude." When broader selections of management occur, frequently there are communication gaps between the lowest- and highest-ranking managers.

Vertical discussions are narrowly focused, in-depth examinations of a department or a division. Examples include the workings of a specific department, how it is organized, where the difficulties lie, where staff works well together and where it does not, and so on. Vertical discussions will involve all levels of management within that department. Participants will include staff and management who are accustomed to working together. Here, because of the daily working relationships, it is possible to involve a broader range of management and staff, but only so long as they stay focused on the narrowly defined subject matter that involves their working together. Thus, an accounts payable departmental discussion on improving efficiency would work well with all management and staff involved. A discussion of restructuring the accounts payable *process* companywide, however, would leave many clerical staff behind.

Diagonal discussions are those that cut across the enterprise and often involve different levels of management, different locations, and different departments. What determines the participant selection is their involvement with the subject matter. Examples would include quality initiatives, areas to improve OSHA safety standards, and obtaining employee reaction and involvement with the selection of a healthcare provider. Often the participants are members of a task force on the given subject matter, another form of diagonal organization.

SEGMENTING THE SUBJECT MATTER FOR DISCUSSION

Without proper structure, CSA sessions could become a long discussion of matters of interest to the organization. It would be a linear discussion with no particular structure, and most likely it would meander into all different kinds of problems, only some of which are of interest to the session sponsors.

Therefore, the CSA session must be organized to become more disciplined, more focused, and more interesting to the participants and to the eventual recipients of the information. This is accomplished by segmenting the entire discussion into smaller, more digestible conversations. Segmenting can be based on two approaches:

1. Breaking up the subject matter according to its component parts, such as the elements of a business process diagram as shown in Exhibit 4.4.
2. Focusing the discussion, and dividing it, into elements derived from some type of external framework that is aligned with the session's objectives. For example, a business risk model, such as the one shown in Exhibit 4.5, can be used to guide the discussion.

By far the easiest way to segment a discussion is to break it up according to its process elements, since these are more natural for the participants to understand and work within.

Using the manufacturing example, the following items would likely be the major discussion segments for a CSA session:

Exhibit 4.4   Major Process Segments

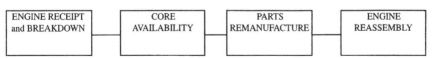

ENGINE RECEIPT and BREAKDOWN	CORE AVAILABILITY	PARTS REMANUFACTURE	ENGINE REASSEMBLY

Exhibit 4.5   Example of a Business Risk Model

Financial Operations	**Product Operations**	**Employee**
Credit Availability	Product Quality	Commitment
Interest Rates	Business Interruption	Efficiency
		Honesty

	Information Risk	
Product Information	Business Information	Market Information

	External Risk	
Legal	Capital Markets	Acts of God
Economic	Competition	Regulation

- o Engine receipt and breakdown
- o Core availability
- o Parts remanufacture
- o Engine reassembly

These major blocks define the manufacturing process of this organization at the highest level. Since our fictitious session is focused on manufacturing process risks, it will not be necessary to examine other processes that affect the company.

The value of segmenting the full CSA session into these smaller pieces includes:

- o Having shorter, closed-end discussions on particular issues
- o Keeping participants' attention levels higher
- o Keeping the discussion focused on specific, not general, issues

Once the session's segments have been agreed upon, the major remaining tasks in planning the session are determining the appropriate questions and writing the session agenda.

DETERMINING THE APPROPRIATE QUESTIONS

At first glance, it may seem obvious to a new CSA practitioner what questions need to be asked. But there is an art to creating a series of questions that will get people to open up, to share information, and to reveal issues that may not have been discussed before.

From this author's experience, CSA questions within each segment follow a similar pattern. For the typical four-question pattern, repeated for each major process segment, the pattern is as follows:

1. *Introduction:* How does this work?
2. *Positive issues (opener):* What is successful here?
   - Deepens participants' knowledge and recall of the subject matter
3. *Negative issues (The "money question"):* What is not working well?
   - The key question you have been leading up to: Where are the problems?
4. *Recommendations:* How to fix the problems?
   - A short discussion of immediate thoughts, no deeper. Then move to the next topic.

This question sequence has proven successful in all CSA sessions conducted by the author. Each question plays a psychological role that is necessary for the outcome, and the sequence of the questions is successful in "opening" the participants to share all information, both positive and negative. An example, based on the engine remanufacturing company, follows. Here the process subject matter is engine receipt and breakdown.

Introductory Question: "How are engines received and broken down?"

Notice that this question is simple and innocuous—it simply asks participants to describe the work process that is known to them all. Their discussion of this process, however, opens the door to further communications. Participants who may have been fearful of speaking now are confident that they can discuss a subject well known to them. The topic also gets the group into a communicative frame of mind. Finally, certain comments will demonstrate the "multiperspective effect," that even the simplest information may be viewed differently by different people. This will be important for later discussions, where participants will encounter different viewpoints on more controversial issues.

Positive Issues: "What is successful here?"

Continuing along the easy-to-contribute path, this question asks participants for specific information on what is working well. The momentum from the first question continues in a nonthreatening way, now asking for observations regarding the successes achieved. Participants have little difficulty in continuing the conversation along these lines, since they are comfortable with discussing positive aspects of situations or processes. This question, however, is setting the stage for the next question—the so-called money question, where the real value of the session begins.

Negative Issues: "What are the problems here?"

By this point, nearly all participants have said something in response to the first two questions. The ice has been broken, and the business process is now being analyzed. Initial feelings of nervousness, intentions not to participate, or other inhibiting factors have been decreased. Now, when the question is asked regarding problems, the participants see this as a natural sequence—if one is to discuss what is right, it is obvious that the next question is what is wrong.

The responses to this question are the basis of any business process improvement. If the first question took 10 minutes, and the second question took 20 minutes, at least 30 to 40 minutes should be devoted to this question. Here specifics should be sought and varying opinions solicited. Most important, the issues raised should be recorded in an on-line session transcript. (See Chapter 10 for more information on session transcripts and templates for recording comments.)

It is also normal for discussions to become involved, controversial, and sometimes heated during the what's-wrong phase of a CSA session. That is most often due to participants' unwillingness to admit that the process is not working successfully or to avoid blame for its lack of success. Here it is critical that the facilitator keep all comments on an impersonal plane and prevent finger-pointing. The facilitator should announce ground rules at the beginning of each session and also whenever a session becomes personal and accusatory: The purpose of the CSA meeting is to determine what is wrong and how to fix it, not whose fault it is. (See Exhibit 9.2 for sample ground rules.)

Recommendations: "How can we fix these problems/resolve these issues?"

Once the "problem question" has been fully answered and participants have had ample time to discuss their perspectives on the issues, the question on recommendations is anticlimactic. Most of the problem responses have a solution recommendation built into them; for example, "insufficient worker training" immediately suggests that training funds and hours be increased. Also, the main energy of the group has been expended on responding to the problem question, and there is little energy left to start inventing solutions. So, in a CSA session, as opposed to other types of sessions (e.g., strategic planning), the solution of problems becomes a relatively short sequence of top-of-the-mind suggestions.

Nevertheless, asking for recommendations is a necessary step in the facilitation process, for it "detunes" the controversy and possible hostilities that emerge during the problem question phase.

Therefore, to leave the group in a neutral, noncontroversial mental state, it is necessary to ask for recommendations and discuss them to a limited extent.

The participants' recommendations may or may not be of significant value: By this point, they are tired and have already contributed most of the solution by defining the problem issues clearly. Of course, all solutions and recommendations should be examined while the group is assembled. Any solution discussed and supported during a group session will be more easily implemented by members of that group.

In summary, the CSA questions do not have to be verbatim copies of the ones proposed here. But the sequence just set forth works well in entering a new discussion, relaxing the participants, getting the easy—and then the hard—information contributed, and then completing the subject matter through recommendations. It is a sequence that works well on both the informational and psychological planes.

CREATING THE SESSION AGENDA

Once the session design has advanced to this stage, subject matter has been segmented, and questions have been created, it is time to plan the actual meeting agenda. There are two purposes for this agenda: informing the participants, and keeping the facilitator on focus and on schedule.

There are few major decisions involved in creating the agenda. It is simply a codification of the information already prepared, but set to a time schedule.

Exhibits 4.6 and 4.7 show typical agendas and are presented in two forms, the agenda for participants and the agenda for the CSA team and facilitator.

Note that the participants' agenda is simple to follow, with little detail. Where there is a reference (e.g., to logistics), the facilitator's agenda provides the detail. This is both to simplify the document for participants and to leave the agenda free to change at the last minute.

Exhibit 4.6   Sample CSA Meeting Agenda for Participants

XYZ Company
Participants' Agenda
Control Self-Assessment Meeting
Meeting Agenda

Meeting Starts at 8:30 A.M.

Breaks will be as follows:

10:00 Morning Break: 15 minutes

12:00 Lunch: 30 minutes

3:00 Afternoon Break: 15 minutes

1. Welcome and Introduction
  A. Logistics of Today's Meeting
  B. Project Objectives
  C. Today's Meeting Objectives
  D. Risk Survey Results

II. Overview of Meeting Process
  A. Risks Suggested, Defined, Discussed
  B. Specific Questions for Each Risk
  C. Anonymous Voting to Determine Most Serious Risks

III. Discussion and Voting of Business Risks
  A. Engine Business Risks
  B. Components Business Risks
  C. Fuel System and Electrics Business Risks
  D. Core Logistics Business Risks
  E. Logistics Operation Business Risks
  F. Strategic Business Risks

IV. Voting Comparison of Business Unit Risk Categories

V. Conclusion
  A. Questions Regarding CSA Process
  B. Next Steps

Meeting Concludes at 4:00 P.M.

Exhibit 4.7   Facilitator's Planning Agenda

XYZ Company
Internal Facilitator's Agenda
Control Self-Assessment Meeting

Meeting Starts at 9:00 A.M.

Introduction Phase: 15–30 minutes

I. (Key Client Sponsor) Welcome participants, establish purpose/importance of session Sponsor then passes meeting to CSA team:

(CSA Team Leader) Welcome and Introduction

A. Logistics of Today's Meeting
   1. 8:00 A.M. to 2:00 P.M.
   2. Telephone/rest room information
   3. Coffee/lunch arrangements
   4. Introduce CSA team personnel and their roles

B. Project Objectives
   1. Overview of Business Risk Model and Assessment Process
   2. Objectives that establish context for Business Risks Company's business objectives discussed
   3. Business Risk Definitions
      a. All risks defined by threat to achieving objectives
      b. Importance for both audit and product planning purposes

C. Today's Meeting Objectives
   Understand, Discuss, and Measure (by voting) Division's Business Risks

D. Risk Survey Results
   1. Number of people surveyed
   2. Reviewed, sorted, combined, and consolidated results into _____ risks within _____ categories and subcategories
   3. Seeking Input/opinion/knowledge on risks and level of resources and controls currently in place for all identified risks
   4. Importance of individual perceptions in measuring risks and "controls" (Define "controls" broadly as having a business purpose)

E. Introduce CSA Team and Facilitator

Process Explanation Phase: 15 minutes

II. (CSA Session Facilitator) Overview of Meeting Process

A. Risk Categorization

continues

Exhibit 4.7   Continued

---

      1. Describe presurvey process

         _____ # of risks, forming _____ # of categories

         Note: Categories are listed according to survey results, not by the Business Risk Model.

      2. Process for Each Business Unit Discussion

         a. Hand out consolidated list of risks for each discussion.

         b. Participants review listing.

         c. Are the presurvey responses clear, meaningful, and appropriate?

         d. Clarify meanings of listed risks.

         e. Add risks that may have been omitted (or clarify as included).

         f. Move on to next discussion.

  B. Questions for Each Risk

      1. What are the elements of this business unit's process?

      2. Where is the process successful? what is working right?

      3. What risks can hinder this business unit from achieving its objectives?

         a. Some risks come from presurvey responses.

         b. Other risks developed in facilitated discussion of process: Outside-the-box risks as well as traditional ones. Check for "handoff risks" in business process

      4. What controls or business solutions are in place today to keep these risks from occurring or from causing serious damage?

  C. Voting Techniques to be Used During session

      1. Will vote risk control map (1–9 voting on both axes)

         a. "Level of Risk" = perception of threat

         b. "Effectiveness of Controls" = how well dealt with or controlled

      2. Participants' knowledge justifies their voting on risk perceptions.

      3. Explain demographics questions.

      4. Show sample risk control map and interpretation template (slide).

<u>Facilitation Phase of Self-Assessment: 5 hours</u>

III. Discussion and Voting of Risks (1 hour each)

  A. Engine Business Risks

  B. Components Business Risks

  C. Fuel System Business Risks

  D. Core Logistics Business Risks

  E. Logistics Operation Business Risks

  F. Strategic Business Risks

---

continues

Exhibit 4.7   Continued

IV. Voting Comparison of Division Business Areas (15 minutes)
   Use pair-comparison voting to determine true priority rankings.

Summary Phase: 15 minutes

   V. (CSA Team Leader) Conclusion

   A. Questions Regarding Process

   B. Next Steps
      1. Analyze results of meeting to develop final, prioritized list of risks.
      2. Focus on resource allocation and controls for highest-priority risks.
      3. Perform gap analysis: risks versus level of controls and resources.
      4. Develop risk profile
      5. Hand out early printed results from today's meeting:
         a. Group risk control map
         b. Consensus maps and/or demographic maps, as appropriate
         c. Personal/confidential client maps

Meeting is then turned over to key client sponsor.
Client sponsor thanks participants for their time and valuable input. (Commitment can be made to provide final reports on session to participants within two to three weeks.)

Meeting Concludes at 4:00 P.M.

Notice also that the first things attended to are the times of the meeting, meal arrangements, and time for breaks and telephone calls (most important). Session attendees need to understand this external structure of the meeting before proceeding to the subject matter itself.

Other points to note:

o This agenda is taken from the same engine remanufacturing company example used previously in this chapter. (However, the breakdown of the remanufacturing process has more elements than discussed earlier.)

o In this engagement, participants were presurveyed via written documents, to fill in what business risks they saw in each major process. This was done to save time during the session and to provide material that would add value to their discussions.

○ Note: The use of the phrase "business risk" in this context is simply to identify what might go wrong in the remanufacturing process. This session actually is focused on business process improvement. In the next chapter we discuss a higher-perspective examination of corporate business risks, which elicits all factors that might threaten the organization's business, both internal and external.

○ Electronic voting was used in the session and is referred to in the agenda. This will be explained further later in the book.

5

Planning a Control Self-Assessment Session to Assess Business Risk

BUSINESS RISK: A SPECIAL PERSPECTIVE

Business process analysis discussions involve the following seven steps:

1. Understanding the purpose of the study
2. Creating an appropriate script of questions
3. Selecting an appropriate group of participants
4. Developing a process diagram specific to the subject matter
5. Breaking down each subprocess into its component parts
6. Inquiring about the inputs, operations, and outputs of each component part and the business process as a whole
7. Reviewing results, making suggestions, and implementing improvements

Exhibit 5.1 presents the process diagram shown in the last chapters, as it is appropriate in a manufacturing context.

Exhibit 5.1   Engine Remanufacture Process Framework

ENGINE RECEIPT and BREAKDOWN	CORE AVAILABILITY	PARTS REMANUFACTURE	ENGINE REASSEMBILY
PARTS CLEANING and RECOVERY	INTERNAL CORE AVAILABILITY	NEW PARTS PURCHASE	
	OPEN MARKET CORE AVAILABILITY		ENGINE TEST and SHIP
			CUSTOMER DELIVERY / CUSTOMER BILLING

Business risk analysis, however, involves a slightly different approach. To begin with, the business risk schematic involves *cause and effect,* not input-operation-output. Exhibit 5.2 develops these ideas a bit further.

Risk, by its very nature, is a matter of possibilities and probabilities. Therefore, it must involve the analysis of *positive and negative likelihoods.* See Exhibit 5.3.

Notice that for every event there are positive and negative causes as well as positive and negative effects. The right inputs can

Exhibit 5.2   Business Process Events

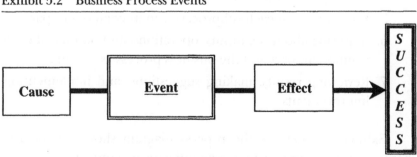

Exhibit 5.3   Business Process Possibilities

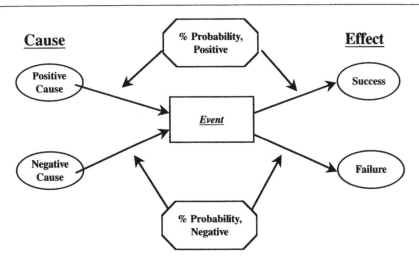

fail, as in mechanical breakdowns, and the wrong inputs can fail to negatively occur, as in overaged machinery continuing to operate.

One more element of this equation is the notion of probability, which is broken into both positive and negative. Probability is the likelihood of events happening well or badly in terms of organizational success.

With these thoughts in mind, we can identify the elements of business risk as follows:

○ Potential *root causes* of failure to achieve an objective
○ *Adverse consequences* of not achieving the objective
○ *Likelihood of failure* to achieve the objective

The definition is illustrated graphically in Exhibit 5.4.

Business risk analysis has to examine all major "events" (in this case, business processes) in an organization, and ask:

○ What are the possible failure events? What can cause them?
○ What are the possible success events? What can hinder them?

Exhibit 5.4   Business Process Risk Events

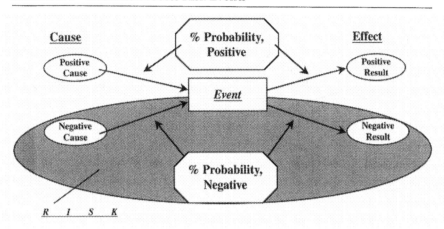

- How likely is it that the failure events will happen?
- How likely is it that the success events will fail to happen?
- What can we do to lessen the likelihood of a failure event, or the likelihood of a success event failing to happen?

Obviously, this analysis is not mathematical, statistical, or physical. It cannot be measured by "risk meters" or mechanical gauges. The only way to estimate the level of risk in a complex situation is to *ask those who are involved with the business process*. Then, by obtaining a representative cross-sample of opinion, one can form a reasonable estimate of the level of business risk.

This chapter, therefore, will define and demonstrate the conduct of a CSA meeting devoted to analyzing business risk. Generally speaking, the questions just listed define the discussion topics led by the facilitator. The only major remaining issue is how to segment the discussion, a topic previously discussed in Chapter 4.

HIGH-LEVEL VIEW: CONTROL SELF-ASSESSMENT AS A BUSINESS RISK ANALYSIS TOOL

The first, most basic, questions to ask in designing a CSA session are:

- What is the subject matter to be examined?
- How shall we organize the discussion to make it easy to follow, easy to participate in, and more "digestible" for participants?
- Who should be invited to the session? (Note that this question must follow the first two, since the subject matter and organization will lead to the necessary participants.)

There are many different ways to approach the second question, how to organize the CSA session. This chapter describes a general approach; then an example from a real session that followed a more customized organization is provided. Once the basic questions have been answered, the session must be "tuned" to meet the client's needs.

The basic dimensions involved in such tuning are shown in Exhibit 5.5.

Time Allotted for Session(s)

Most CSA sessions will be severely time-limited, due to participants' work responsibilities. This, however, has to be balanced against the importance of the CSA subject matter to the organization as a whole. Typically, a single, four- to six-hour meeting can be scheduled on a subject, although there will still be a need to convince management personnel to attend. (Shopfloor personnel can attend more easily when required, since typically they require only a supervisor's permission to do so.)

The difficulty facilitators will face is obtaining this time, particularly if multiple meetings are required. It is therefore rec-

Exhibit 5.5   The Five Planning Dimensions

---

1. **Time allotted for session(s)**
2. **Breadth of coverage (scope)**
3. **Depth of detail**
4. **Coverage of cross-section of employees**
5. **Sufficient data to cross-validate results**

ommended that the subject matter be organized in a way that will enable the CSA sessions to be held over a series of weeks, with each session handling one specific subset of the topic to be discussed.

As an example, consider an enterprisewide examination of business risk. Here successive sessions might be organized as follows in a manufacturing environment:

Session 1: General Overview of Internal Corporate Business Risks Participants: CEO and all vice-presidents

Session 2: In-depth Discussion of Financial Risks
Participants: VP of Finance, key financial managers

Session 3: In-depth Discussion of Manufacturing Processs Risks
Participants: VP of Manufacturing, key manufacturing managers

Session 4: In-depth Discussion of Logistics Risks
Participants: VP of Logistics, key logistics managers

Session 5: In-depth Discussion of External Business Risks
Participants: CEO + key VPs and senior managers

All sessions should be of the same length, probably four to six hours, and should be scheduled in advance to enable participants to plan their calendars. A separation of one to two weeks is recommended: a minimum of one week to enable participants to get their work done and absorb the information from the last meeting; no more than two weeks, so that the information does not become stale. Also, if a session achieves its goals in a lesser time, it should be dismissed early out of respect for participants' other responsibilities.

Breadth of Coverage (Scope)

Breadth of coverage (together with the next item, depth of detail) presents the most serious conflict with participants' time availability.

It is strongly recommended that session planners try to narrow the scope of their inquiry severely, for two reasons:

1. A well-defined and narrow scope will help ensure an efficient, rewarding session for participants.
2. An overbroad session will be dull for participants, and it will be clear that the subject matter was poorly chosen. This, in turn, will lessen participants' willingness to attend future sessions.

Broad areas and large issues can be examined, but each CSA session should be designed appropriately. This moves the planning effort to the next item: depth of detail.

Depth of Detail

Within a given subject matter, depth of detail must always be balanced against breadth of coverage. You cannot have both without extending the time required for sessions. Therefore, if a broad area must be examined, CSA sponsors will have to agree to higher-level results or, if absolutely necessary to get detailed answers, to extend the CSA project into multiple sessions.

Usually, however, management understands the value of higher-level data. In most cases, what is being sought is guidance as to the most important issues or problems facing a company, with some recommendations as to how to proceed with solutions. In very rare cases when client sponsors insist on *both* breadth and depth, they find it difficult to schedule longer meetings (e.g., two to three days) or multiple sessions with senior management. Essentially, this becomes an exercise in self-discipline: "You can't always get what you want," as the song says.

Coverage of Cross-Section of Employees

This issue and the next one, cross-validation, are secondary to the three just described. They both focus on the validity of the data from the sessions, to ensure that it is correct and supportable.

The employees in a session (or a series of sessions) need to satisfy two requirements:

1. They need to be sufficiently knowledgeable in the matters discussed, so as to guarantee the accuracy of the results to management.
2. They need to represent a sufficient cross-section of the organization that the results obtained will represent an accurate cross-organizational picture.

A lesser aspect of this issue is the nonattendance of key participants. From a session planning perspective, two types of participants are critical to the outcome:

1. Those who are involved with the issues and knowledgeable of the problems
2. Those who will be necessary to implementing likely solutions to those problems

If a key person from either of these groups cannot attend, the quality of the data or the likelihood of solution implementation is threatened. Therefore, all possible effort must be made to ensure the willing (not grudging) attendance of all key participants.

Finally, there is one other issue regarding the selection and attendance of key participants: If one or more key players is missing from the group, it will be very difficult for them to later understand the perspectives shared during the meeting. This, in turn, will make it difficult for nonattendees to fully support the session's recommendations and to assist in the implementation of those plans.

Data Sufficient to Cross-Validate Results

In many situations, participants will "know" or "have a gut feeling" that there is a problem or that a solution would work in solving it. Usually, given the experience of these internal experts, that is sufficient.

However, some situations will require that the answers be validated. Validation will require one of the following approaches:

o Adding to the number of participants, to obtain a large range of views.

o Lengthening the session, to ensure that the issues are discussed in sufficient, detailed depth

o Having multiple sessions, to ensure that similar results are obtained in different settings

If one of these approaches is necessary, the facilitator must examine the importance of the issue, and the cost and inconvenience of adding more participants or allocating more time.

Balancing the Five Planning Dimensions

The five dimensions just described all affect each other and, even more important, affect the budget allocated for the CSA project. Therefore, at the very beginning of a project, these five dimensions must be specifically discussed among the CSA team and brought to the client's attention.

When planning a CSA session or project, therefore, it is critical that members of the CSA team agree on each of these and put them into writing for management's review. Client sponsors typically want to "have it all," until they are shown the cost and complexity of what "it all" requires. A written session planning document, therefore, is necessary to reveal these issues to the sponsors and to initiate a discussion as to which dimensions are primary and which are secondary.

Once the planning dimensions are agreed between the CSA team and sponsor(s), it is recommended that these agreed objectives be put into writing and communicated to the client sponsor. The key sponsor should review the document with management to ensure that they all understand and agree with the agreed priorities for the session(s).

DESIGNING A CONTROL SELF-ASSESSMENT SESSION AGENDA

Once these issues have been agreed upon, the next task is to design the actual session agenda. A number of approaches can be used:

- ○ A generic design approach
- ○ An approach that reflects the problem issues
- ○ An approach that reflects the organization's structure
- ○ An approach that is based on some type of CSA framework (discussed in Chapter 6)
- ○ An approach that combines two or more of the above

We will illustrate a generic design formula that can provide a first-draft session design.

Generic Design Approach

There is a method for developing a simple, high-perspective CSA agenda with nearly any subject matter. It involves a four-step formula and is simple to use.

Step 1: Develop a Clear Statement of the Assessment Objective. This is a clear necessity, whether using the generic design formula or not. Before any session can take place, it is essential that the client and the facilitator/consulting team know the purpose of the session. In an engagement where there are numerous sessions, it will be necessary to have a well-defined engagement objective; however, each CSA session will need to also have its own assessment objective defined and agreed with the client. An example of such objectives is shown in Exhibit 5.6.

For this client, business operations are fully described by four separate processes: raw materials purchasing, manufacturing, marketing and sales, and distribution of the finished product. Each process will be examined in detail in a four- to six-hour CSA session, and each session will be designed using the generic design approach.

Exhibit 5.6   Sample Assessment Objectives—Step 1

Engagement Objective: Determine process inefficiencies in the materials purchasing, manufacture, sale, and distribution of widgets.

- Session #1 Assessment Objective: Review the raw materials purchasing
  process for potential inefficiencies.
- Session #2 Assessment Objective: Review the widget manufacturing
  process for potential inefficiencies.
- Session #3 Assessment Objective: Review the marketing and sales process
  for potential inefficiencies.
- Session #4 Assessment Objective: Review the distribution process for
  potential inefficiencies.

*Step 2: Segment the Full Meeting into Three to Five Smaller Discussion
Segments.* For each of the four CSA meetings, the process under
examination will be subdivided into three to five segments. For the
marketing and sales process, for example, these segments will be:

- Market research
- Marketing communications
- Sales prospecting
- Sales presentations
- Sales closing

The manufacturing process, as another example, could have
the following segments:

- Materials preparation
- Metal-forming
- Parts assembly
- Finishing

Notice that these segments are natural and logical overviews of
the process. It is not necessary at this point to have highly detailed

process flow diagrams, although it will be helpful to have them in each session for reference.

Step 3: Develop Specific Questions to Ask in Each Discussion Segment.[1] This is the step that instills the greatest fear in CSA facilitators: "How will I determine which questions to ask?" The answer is simple: *The questions will follow a basic sequence of three to four questions and will relate directly to the assessment objective.* Typically, the questions are logical derivations of the assessment objective. They could even be developed by envisioning a one-on-one interview about the process with a senior manager.

Usually a series of four questions, asking for increasingly important process insights, is used. An overview of the four-question series for manufacturing is as follows:

1. What is this process segment (e.g., materials preparation)? Describe how it works.
2. What is right with this process segment? Tell where it is successful.
3. What is wrong with this process segment? Tell where it is broken.
4. What should be done to fix or improve this process segment? Suggest remedial steps.

Note that these questions form a sequence that delves deeper and deeper into the subject matter. The questions start on a simple, easy-to-answer level: How does it work? This question seeks information for the record, but it also serves as an "ice-breaker" for the group. By seeking noncontroversial information, they are free to join in the discussion without criticizing various elements of the business process.

The second question is positive and therefore easier to answer by participants: What is right with the process? Most people find it easier to answer questions that are seeking positive or "good" information, and this second question gives participants an opportunity to start the discussion on a positive level. With the momentum created by the first question as well as the positive thrust of the second question, the group should be fully contributing to the session. The scribe should now be recording numerous comments, giving deeper and deeper details on the process or subprocess in question.

The third question—"What is wrong with this process?"—is the most important of the four-question series. This is the "money question," the part of the CSA process where the most valuable data are obtained. It is relatively easy to ask this question after the group has exhausted the subject of "What's right?" since they will expect to be asked for negatives when done with the positives. From a group dynamic perspective, they are now fully involved in the discussion and have developed some conversational momentum. They are also comfortable with the subject matter, since many group members will have learned about the process under discussion from other participants' comments.

Once the third question has been fully answered and group responses have slowed down, the final question is remedial: "What can be done to fix these problems?" This, too, is an outgrowth of the prior question and will have a natural feel for participants. In addition, it will have a restorative effect on the group dynamic, which often slows down or has difficulty when talking about what is wrong with the business process. By asking for potential improvements and remedies, group members have now returned to a positive conversational state. At this point, they are ready to go on to discussing the next process segment.

Step 4: Determine Where and How Electronic Voting Will Be Used. Again, most facilitators have little idea where to start with voting questions. And again, the answer is simple and logical: *Since voting allows people's perceptions to be quantified, what perceptions of the group are critical to achieving the objectives of the meeting?*

As an example, we can look at a session analyzing business risks. What are the perceptual issues for business risks?

○ How big are they?
○ How bad are they?
○ How prepared are we?

Put another way, the formal voting questions might be phrased as follows:

- What level of damage might be caused by this business risk?
- How frequently might this business risk occur?
- How effective are our process controls in regard to this business risk?

These questions were used to create the risk filter map shown in Exhibit 1.5 and the risk control map shown in Exhibit 1.6. Note that the risk filter map asks for potential damage versus likelihood, and the map easily shows the more serious business risks—those in the high-damage/high-likelihood quadrant. The risk control map then is used only on the high-scoring business risks (top-right quadrant) and simply asks, "How much of a *threat* is this risk?" With a brief definition of threat by the facilitator—as simple as "a gut-level feeling of the total danger this poses to the business process"—participants can easily rate threat on a 1-to-9 scale or similar standard. The same "gut-level" estimation can be used to estimate the effectiveness of the process controls, and the resulting map averages out the entire group's perceptions of the issue for each and every business risk listed.

Summary of the Four-Step Generic Design Approach

Using the above approach, we now have been able to take an unfamiliar subject and build a CSA agenda for a full-day meeting to examine the marketing and sales process of the enterprise. There will be five separate discussion segments:

1. Market research
2. Marketing communications
3. Sales prospecting
4. Sales presentations
5. Sales closing

Each discussion segment will ask the same four questions:

1. What is this process segment (e.g., market research)? Describe how it works.
2. What is right with this process segment? Tell where it is successful.
3. What is wrong with this process segment? Tell where it is broken.
4. What should be done to fix or improve this process segment? Suggest remedial steps.

At the end of each segment, electronic voting will be used to ask the questions:

○ What level of damage might be caused by this business risk?
○ How frequently might this business risk occur?
○ How effective are our process controls in regards to this business risk?

The answers to these questions will enable the group to develop two key maps, the risk filter map and the risk control map, for each process segment.

Without question, this agenda will obtain valuable information in a relatively short period of time. Each process segment should have one to one and a half hours for discussion, and the day's transcription and voting data will provide management with significant insight into the business risks associated with the process under examination.

Most important, the same generic design approach can be used with nearly any business process problem that a facilitator will encounter.

NOTE

[1] This Step 3 description is a brief summary of "Determining the Appropriate Questions" in Chapter 4.

6

Importance of Frameworks

CHOOSING THE RIGHT FRAMEWORK

Control Self-Assessment is more than a simple discussion. Rather, it is a structured process, focused on a particular subject matter and *guided by an agreed framework*. The nature of the framework will vary with each engagement or assignment. Sometimes the framework will be explicit; sometimes it will be implicit. But all CSA sessions have a framework, whether in foreground or background mode.

Examples of CSA frameworks may include any of the following:

- A business process model
- A framework relating to the particular project
- A framework that describes the purpose of the meeting (rather than the subject matter under examination)
- A business risk model
- An internal audit control model

Some frameworks are immediately useful in guiding a CSA session. A business process model, for example, sets forth explicitly which are the major processes of a business, which are the subprocesses, and how these processes (at all levels) relate to each other. This type of framework is a natural starting point for designing a session on the workings of this particular business process.

There are other session objectives, however, that may look at the same business process from a different perspective, such as quality improvement. In such a case, there are two frameworks to choose from:

1. The business process model
2. The quality improvement model

The quality improvement model is the more likely one to use. This is because the session is primarily focused on quality and secondarily on the particular business process it is being applied to.

Judgments like these are subjective and complex, and often require the input of the client, the CSA team, and possible experts in the field. There will also be occasions when the two (or more) models are combined into a customized meeting framework, used strictly to focus this one CSA session on meeting its objectives.

A BUSINESS PROCESS MODEL

The framework shown in Exhibit 6.1 lends itself easily to a process review CSA session. The business processes are clear and distinct, as are their relationships.

FRAMEWORK RELATING TO THE PARTICULAR PROJECT

The framework shown in Exhibit 6.2 was derived from the text of a contract to conduct research on the CSA process. It was the basis of the author's prior book on this subject, *Control Self-Assessment— Experience, Current Thinking and Best Practices*. Exhibit 6.2 is the high-level framework of the full research project. Exhibit 6.3 depicts the more detailed questions to be asked in each of the three major research areas.

This shows the direct application of a project framework to conducting a CSA session: in the research sessions, questions were asked in the order provided by the project model.

Exhibit 6.1   Engine Remanufacture Process Framework

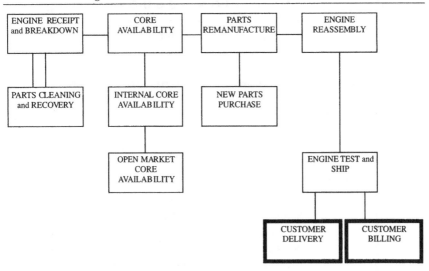

Exhibit 6.2   IIA Control Self-Assessment Research Framework

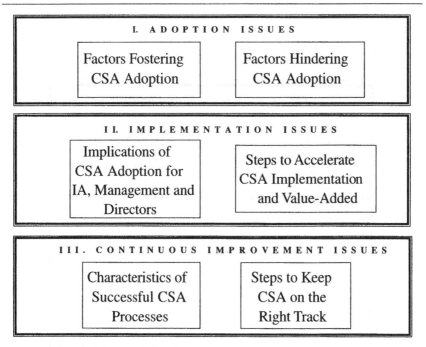

Reprinted with permission from the Institute of Internal Auditors Research Foundation.

Exhibit 6.3   Detailed Project Framework (1 of 3)

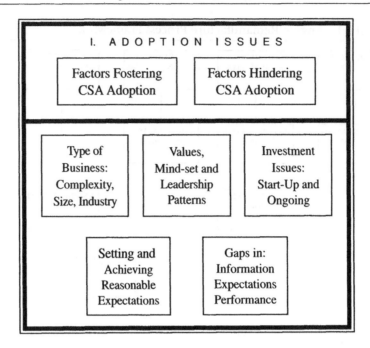

Exhibit 6.3   Detailed Project Framework (2 of 3)

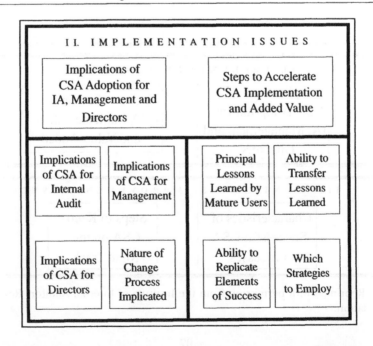

Exhibit 6.3   Detailed Project Framework (3 of 3)

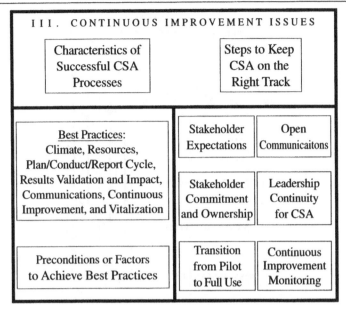

Reprinted with permission from the Institute of Internal Auditors Research Foundation.

INTERNAL AUDIT CONTROL MODELS

In the internal audit field, the role of a control model is to provide a complete listing of audit risks that may be encountered. Control models may be the COSO model (for "Committee of Sponsoring Organizations" of the Treadway Commission Report, which generated it), in the United States, the CoCo model (Criteria of Control) in Canada, the Internal Control and Financial Reporting study in the United Kingdom, or a framework or set of objectives customized for a specific organization (e.g., a customized business controls framework). Because selection of the control model reflects management's control objectives, it is important to understand that the self-assessment approach can be used to help comply with any control model. The key issue is whether the control model is used later to organize the information gained from CSA meetings, or whether it is used as the structure of the CSA meeting itself.

Exhibit 6.4   The COSO Model for Internal Controls

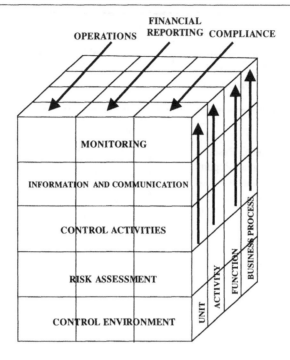

The model shown in Exhibit 6.4 is the COSO model, used extensively in the United States.

There has been little success in using the COSO model as a framework for CSA business discussions because the categories are overly abstract for the business participants. A successful session should be more concrete in its subject matter, focused on specific business issues. Following a broadly focused model to ensure complete coverage will guarantee a lengthy and difficult session for participants.

The CoCo Model, shown in Exhibit 6.5, serves essentially the same purpose as the COSO model. However, it looks at the issue of audit controls from a time sequence rather than an organizational perspective. In other words, the CoCo model analyzes control in the chronological order of the steps taken to accomplish any corporate objective.

Exhibit 6.5   The CoCo Model for "Criteria of Control"

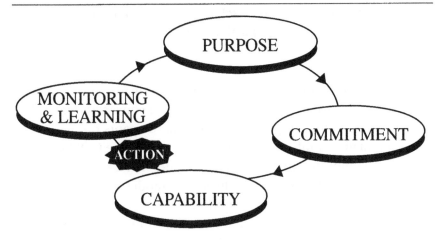

The CoCo model is described at the Web site of the Canadian Institute of Chartered Accountants (CICA) as follows[1]:

> *"How does the CoCo model deal with control?"*
>
> "In any organization of people, the essence of *control* is the blending of *purpose, commitment, capability,* and *monitoring* and *learning.*
>
> "A person performs a task, guided by an understanding of its *purpose* (the objective to be achieved) and supported by *capability* (information, resources, supplies and skills). The person will need a sense of *commitment* to perform the task well over time. The person will *monitor* his or her performance and the external environment to *learn* how to do the task better and about changes to be made. The same is true of any team or work group."

From an auditor's perspective, both models are effective in ensuring that a business enterprise has sufficient controls on operations and processes. From a CSA facilitator's viewpoint, however, the models are vastly different:

○ The COSO model is useful after a CSA session, to categorize the information elicited.

o The CoCo model, on the other hand, is highly useful in organizing the session itself—the sequence of questions, the discussion among participants, and the major issues addressed.

The CoCo model has a natural flow that mirrors the sequence of work activities. This allows it to be used in a conversational, informal meeting, asking simple questions of participants but gathering the same quality of information as is suggested in the COSO model. The CICA committee that created the model had a number of CSA pioneers among its members. The CoCo model was intentionally designed to be useful in CSA meetings.

The lesson, therefore, is that frameworks or models should be chosen carefully. Never assume that a proposed model, however well regarded, will serve as the backbone for a CSA session. Work with participants and clients to develop a framework that is meaningful and helpful, and then use it consistently to elicit the information needed.

A Business Risk Model

The framework depicted in Exhibit 6.6 is used to classify various elements of business risk that have been encountered in a risk management engagement. The advantage of this framework is that it is comprehensive, similar to library classification systems such as the Dewey Decimal System. The disadvantage also relates to its comprehensiveness: The framework is so broad that it cannot be used as a checklist for a CSA session.

IMPORTANCE OF CONTROL SELF-ASSESSMENT TO FRAMEWORKS

Although frameworks hold a special role in the planning of CSA sessions, CSA offers its own value to business frameworks and models. Up to now, many such frameworks have been proposed and adopted in an organization's business structure, but it has been

Exhibit 6.6   Example of a Business Risk Model

Financial Operations	**Product Operations**	**Employee**
Credit Availability	Product Quality	Commitment
Interest Rates	Business Interruption	Efficiency
		Honesty

	Information Risk	
Product	Business	Market
Information	Information	Information

	External Risk	
Legal	Capital Markets	Acts of God
Economic	Competition	Regulation

difficult to analyze the business enterprise strictly according to the particular model used.

Now, using CSA a group's discussion can be structured easily to fit a specific framework. Some frameworks may allow more "natural" discussions, such as a manufacturing process model; others may offer an abstract framework, such as the COSO model. Whether concrete or abstract, any framework can help in organizing a CSA meeting and providing management with exactly the information sought to improve business performance or control business risks.

Therefore, when a CSA project has been proposed, the CSA team should immediately seek out existing models and frameworks appropriate to the subject matter. They may well find that their session(s) will flow better using these background structures, that questions will be easier to formulate, and that participants will understand the purpose of the meeting and its results more easily.

NOTE

[1] URL: http://www.cica.ca/new/ss/e_cocoov.htm. Also see *Control and Guidance for Directors; Governance Processes for Control* (Toronto: Canadian Institute of Chartered Accountants, 1997).

7

Using Facilitation as a Consulting Sales Tool

INTRODUCTION

Up to this point, we have examined facilitation—including both the strategic approach and the Control Self-Assessment methodology—as a tool for conducting consulting engagements. Facilitation, however, can be used in a different context: to develop new sales opportunities through a presales facilitation session.

This application of facilitation is little known in the general marketplace, but has been developed and proven by the author in two different scenarios:

1. Client marketing seminars, involving numerous companies' executives
2. Engagement scoping sessions for new clients prospects, developing their specific needs for a consulting engagement and leading to a formal proposal

Note that in this chapter, we shall be using a "future planning" facilitation methodology. This involves the use of flipcharts, rather than electronic scribing, and provides a creative environment for the idea-generation share of the meeting. Note, however, that this is not a CSA methodology.

POTENTIAL FOR FACILITATION-BASED SELLING

A seminar using facilitation can simply demonstrate the power of the facilitation tool, where facilitation-based consulting is the service being marketed, or it can open participants' eyes to the potential benefits of a product or consulting service being promoted. The author has had experience in a number of facilitated marketing seminars. These were conducted for an information systems consulting firm, and were used for two different marketing objectives:

1. "Using Information for Competitive Advantage"—to sell consulting services
2. "Information Sharing for Competitive Advantage"—to sell Lotus Notes, with required implementation services

Note that these titles, although apparently similar, actually generate entirely different discussions. The first focuses on how information can be used to improve a company's position in the market, and produces a list of the types of information that will be needed to achieve this goal. The results of these sessions showed the process used to determine a company's specific information needs, leading to a information plan. This became a model for potential consulting engagements that could be delivered to each of the participating companies.

The second subject, *sharing* information, focuses on the need for an internal communications infrastructure. These seminars were conducted in cooperation with the Lotus Notes sales organization in 1994, which had been having difficulty in positioning Lotus Notes as a higher-level product than corporate e-mail. The purpose of the session was to immerse business executives in the issues of information sharing, so that they would then understand the benefits of an information-sharing tool. One regional sales executive from the Lotus organization later commented, "This is the best way to sell Lotus Notes that I have ever seen."

But how can we get participants from possibly competing companies to discuss issues in an open, collegial manner? By a very simple device—a fictitious conglomerate. A company is postulated (entitled "Mega-Corp" in our sessions) that has acquired all of the participants' own companies and has tasked them to work together within a common business structure. Participants are also given a unifying principle, Mega-Corp's mission statement: "Growth—Through Increased Sales and Increased Profitability." This enables participants to discuss their own issues, but in a Mega-Corp context.

Facilitated marketing seminars are not limited to the specific participants who are involved in the actual discussion. In the examples just provided, there was a full audience (60+ executives), with only 20 executives actually involved in the facilitation. The others observed the session and later asked questions about the process used to obtain such high-quality, immediate results.

CLIENT MARKETING SEMINARS

There are two ways to use facilitation to convert prospects to clients in marketing seminars:

1. Demonstrate the technique and effectiveness of the facilitation technique, to close on a facilitation-based consulting engagement.
2. Use facilitation to demonstrate the client's need for a consulting engagement on certain issues, whether that engagement will use facilitation methodologies or not. This is typically a high-level executive meeting.

When conducting a multicompany session, a group of executives must be involved in a single discussion that has a common importance to them all. The difficulty, assuming that they all share a common problem (e.g., the need for information systems to help achieve competitive advantage), is that these executives represent different and sometimes competing business entities. Therefore, the seminar session must be as effective as possible, without delving into confidential or competitive information.

USING FACILITATION FOR CONSULTING
ENGAGEMENT SALES

When consulting services are required, there is always a problem to be solved. Consulting service sales are based on a "problem-solution" discussion, and include most of the following components:

○ Existence of a problem
○ Agreed-upon definition of the problem
○ Clients' consensus of the problem's priority
○ Consultants' insight into problem solution
○ Demonstrated capability to solve the problem
○ Client management consensus on the proposed engagement approach

The use of a facilitation session, however brief, will help advance all of the above stages of consultative selling. These sessions can be so powerful that some consulting firms will give away a sample session, lasting about three hours. These sessions do not solve the problem, but rather give management the opportunity to hold discussions without interruption by other issues. They also develop client consensus on the importance of the issues, and an excellent relationship with the consulting firm.

Once a session has been held, even a shortened version, the consultative sales agenda has been advanced. This is because the session will deliver, at the very least, management's consensus that there is a problem and probably an agreed-upon definition of what the problem is. Also, if the problem has multiple components, the electronic voting approach will clearly prioritize which aspects of the main problem should be attacked first.

If the consulting organization is able to gain the client's willingness to pay for up-front engagement planning sessions, all the better. Facilitation, whether strategic or CSA, can be used to shorten the engagement interview and planning phase. For a small initial investment, the client and the consulting team can work together to organize a potential engagement.

"Working together" is really the point of up-front facilitations. Once the client team has participated in a facilitation meeting, they have a clearer understanding and consensus of what they need. They also have a strong relationship with the consulting team. Facilitation sessions build relationships quickly, based on the high quality of the discussions that take place. Such sessions are ideal opportunities for a consulting firm to get to know the client and vice versa. From a competitive viewpoint, any consulting firm that can provide a facilitation session to define engagement issues will have a clear advantage over competing firms.

FACILITATION SEMINARS FOR PRODUCT SALES

Although the last example is related to a product (Lotus Notes), facilitation is not typically recommended for product sales. The reason is that, the better the session succeeds in selling a specific product, the more manipulative it will seem to participants. Such a perception will turn participants against the session sponsors, and they will be less likely to buy the product.

There are some exceptions, however. In the Lotus Notes situation, there was a foundational problem: potential customers did not understand the need for information sharing or the potential benefits it could bring to their organizations. Once that understanding was developed, the more complex functionality of Lotus Notes could be explained and justified with a customer audience that was now willing to listen. In other words, the facilitation seminar did not "sell" Lotus Notes. It just provided the information needed for customers to understand whether they had a need for it or not.

Also note that, even though the Lotus organization made a product presentation at the end of the morning's facilitation session, it was only a 15-minute promotion while the facilitation session lasted two-and-one-half hours. This short presentation did not damage the customer goodwill that had been built—after all, Lotus Notes was a cosponsor of the meeting. And it did give an opportunity for seminar participants (both those involved in the facilitation and those observing) to ask questions regarding the potential implementation of an information-sharing product. A proper balance was struck between information and sales, and all parties benefited.

WHICH FACILITATION PROCESS TO USE

Throughout this book, both strategic and CSA forms of facilitation have been described. Their differentiation has been based on whether the session is focused on planning or on process analysis. In the case of sales-oriented facilitation sessions, however, the analysis is quite different.

Strategic facilitation could be simply described as creative problem-solving or idea-building. In contrast, CSA sessions are more focused on finding and fixing what is wrong with the process. In a consulting engagement, both techniques have their place, but in a sales situation, only strategic facilitation should be used.

The simple reason is that people enjoy problem-solving and idea-building far more than analyzing problems. A good strategic facilitation session often ends in applause for the facilitator; however, the author has never heard of applause resulting from a CSA session. The reason is a matter of psychology: Positivity is always preferred over negativity, and people enjoy building ideas far more than discovering problems. In a sales context, therefore, one is far more likely to gain a positive client relationship through the strategic, idea-building form of facilitation.

WHEN CAN A SEMINAR USE CONTROL SELF-ASSESSMENT METHODOLOGY?

The sole exception to the rule to use strategic facilitation in seminars, is when the CSA methodology itself must be demonstrated to show its effectiveness to clients.

As an example, the author was asked to lead a CSA facilitation effort to examine process controls in an engine remanufacturing plant. What resulted was a two-day CSA session involving all key managers at that one plant. The result? Clear recommendations as to which process controls were strongest and weakest, and where the greatest threats to the remanufacturing process were faced. Within its limited objective, the session was a success.

The result of this one session, however, was far greater than the facilitation team expected. Based on the effectiveness of the CSA session with a manufacturing process, the next application for CSA was to analyze financial risks and controls for the entire $6 billion parent company. Client management understood the thoroughness and accuracy of the CSA approach, and valued the voting maps showing participants' views of business risks. They also knew that the same approach would be effective with financial issues.

Thus, a CSA session can demonstrate a larger engagement consulting approach. Readers are encouraged to develop some experience in facilitation and then to experiment with these marketing approaches.

STRATEGIC FACILITATION PROCESS FOR SEMINARS

Pre-session Objective-Setting

The pre-session phase of the session will accomplish these objectives:

- Establish a marketing objective
- Create a group dynamic
- Set the right depth and detail of questions and answers

Establishing a Marketing Objective. The first step to a successful meeting is the creation of a marketing objective. This will be initiated by a written statement, which is discussed and agreed with the client. This objective should satisfy the following criteria for a successful session:

- It should further the sponsor's marketing agenda and should be a subject of interest to the invited audience.
- It should discuss a number of issues that will draw on participants' own experience.

111

- It should be focused at a high level, with a minimum of technical detail.
- Participants' contributions can be integrated into a few, well-defined solution strategies.
- The strategies that are developed will be prioritized through an electronic voting system—a feature of high value to the participants, and one that will leave them with an excellent impression of the session.
- The entire seminar session should take no more than three hours.

The marketing objective is created before the meeting. The first task at the session itself is to ensure that the participants accept the objective—that it truly becomes a *common* objective.

In the following example, the formal marketing objective is as follows:

> Help seminar participants understand the opportunities they have to improve their company's competitive position, through improvements in their information systems. The sales goal is that they will purchase our consulting services within X months of the seminar.

That objective is clearly focused on the sponsor's needs. To be effective in the seminar, it must be restated in a form that focuses on the needs of the audience. Here, using the Mega-Corp example, the participants' *session objective* would be:

> Develop information strategies to improve Mega-Corp's competitive position.

The seminar sponsor has indicated support for this objective prior to the session. Once participants do so, the session can begin.

Setting the Right Depth and Detail of Questions and Answers

This is only a marketing seminar, not a quest for real problems and root causes; therefore, the facilitator must be careful in the depth of questions presented. They should advance the subject-matter agenda but in no way threaten the group's perception of a harmless discussion. Thus, the facilitator should ensure participation that is useful but is not overly revealing of the company's plans.

This means that a certain "altitude-setting" will be necessary at the beginning of the session: If questions or answers have too abstract a perspective to gain useful information, adjustments should be made. On the other hand, if the responses are too detailed and threaten completing the discussion within the allotted three-hour period, the facilitator needs to raise the level of discussion.

The Kick-Off

Creating a Group Dynamic. In all facilitation sessions, it is important to start the session with a statement of the meeting's purpose and then provide an opportunity for participants to introduce themselves to the group. In an intracompany session, this is important while in a marketing seminar, it is critical. The initial go-around-the-room introductions are essential to the formation of a strong group dynamic, even if it is needed only for the duration of the marketing seminar.

Prior to requesting introductory information, establish a proper subject-matter context, one in which the participants could see themselves having a conversation. In our experience, the Mega-Corp device of a fictitious conglomerate has worked well.

As basic as these ideas are, they do provide a context for discussing pertinent issues. One should not, however, support participants' providing confidential or competitive information, and that should be made clear to all at the start of the session. With an agreed-upon expectation of noncompetitive information, most participants will feel comfortable in engaging in these discussions.

An example of a facilitator's session kick-off comments might be as follows: "Good morning, and welcome to Mega-Corp's competitive strategy planning session. The objective of this meeting is to answer the following question: 'What can information systems do to improve Mega-Corp's competitive position?'

"Since each of you come from a different division of Mega-Corp, we'd like to start the session by asking you to introduce yourselves. These self-introductions should include your name and title, the name of your division and what its business focus is, and what you would personally like to achieve in today's session."

The self-introductions go sequentially around the room, with the facilitator writing all personal objectives on a flipchart. No names are written at any time during the session.

At the end of the introductions, the facilitator would say: "I see that we have a broad range of personal objectives, but they seem to fall within the meeting's general objective. Are we all ready to begin our session, keeping both the session objective and our personal objectives in mind?" The usual responses are statements of "yes," either verbally or through head-nods.

At this point the facilitator has achieved the first major objective: the formation of a group dynamic, as shown by members' agreement to participate in the session. This is a critical and necessary step in developing successful and valuable results. There will be little constructive conversation without the individuals' agreement that they support the session's objectives, even in this artificial situation.

Problem Gathering

After the introductory phase is complete, the information gathering begins. The facilitator should have basic questions prepared to find the participants' key problems, such as:

- Is your information system helping your company's business? Why not?
- Have you previously used information resources to improve your competitive position? Where? Was this effective?
- What kind of problems do you perceive in your current information systems?

Participants will tend to get bogged down in detail, or at least try to remain on a single issue to discuss it thoroughly. The facilitator's role is to prevent this. All problems should be summarized briefly (always using flipcharts to record the answers), and then the facilitator should ask the group for other problems.

The other tendency for groups is to attempt to work each problem toward a solution in the initial conversation. This will not work in a facilitation. Problems need to be discussed in one phase and solutions need to be developed in another phase. It will be necessary to advise participants of this approach at the beginning of the session. Paper pads should be provided to participants so they can jot down ideas occurring during the session for use later in the meeting. (Three-by-five-inch Post-it Notes are an excellent tool for this.) Once initial responses have been made, the facilitator should ask frequently, "Any more problems?" or "Anything else?" When the responses get fewer and farther between, the session can move forward to the next phase.

Root Causes Discussion—"Obstacles"

Continuing the session, the facilitator now asks what factors might cause the problems listed in the prior segment of the meeting. These factors are not the problems themselves, they are the "obstacles" or root causes of those problems. Examples might include:

- Lack of sufficient planning
- Lack of funding
- Lack of management support
- Legal barriers

Note that many obstacles start with the phrase "Lack of . . ." It is important that this phase also continue until the obstacles are fully listed. It will be more difficult to generate constructive ideas if the participants have not fully described the problems and the obstacles that created the situation.

Once the obstacles are stated, the group dynamic will be negative and somewhat depressed. That is normal at this stage, and should be so described to the group. Participants should be told that they have reached the end of the "negativity discussion" and are about to enter the positive, solution-oriented phase of the meeting.

Resources Discussion—"Enablers"

Turning toward the positive side of the information systems issues, the facilitator then asks participants to list items that might fix problems or root causes listed previously. This is the converse of root-cause analysis and is focused on root resolutions. Answers that might be heard are:

- Additional funding
- Greater management understanding of the issues
- Greater management support
- More aggressive, customer-oriented thinking by the information systems department

Note that these are not the creative ideas and fixes that the audience is waiting to contribute; rather, these are the building blocks to get to those ideas.

Again, as with all facilitation discussion segments, the facilitator should know when to move on as the pace of answers gets slower and slower.

Creative Idea Generation

There should be a short break, no more than 10 minutes, for participants to stretch and refresh themselves before this phase of the meeting. It should not be used for telephone calls, since often calls break up participants' concentration on the meetings subject matter. Creative idea generation is the core of the strategic facilitation process. It consists of the development of original ideas by individual participants, ideas that are later combined into strategies for improving the company's business success. Note also that the strategic session is future-oriented. The mechanism for establishing that future orientation is described on the next page.

Now the group will reap the benefits of the earlier, negative discussions that started the session, the problems and obstacles. These statements were written on flipchart pages and hung along the walls. Now these pages will become a resource for creativity.

The Future-Pull Question

First, the facilitator should acknowledge how hard the participants have worked and the quality of their input to the session. Then comes the introduction to the key question that the group will be asked to answer. The facilitator's comments might be as follows. "Now that all the problems and root causes have been stated and the potential enablers listed, we'd like you to move your thinking forward in time. Imagine, if you will, that this is the year [a date five years in the future] and Mega-Corp has just received the Presidential Award for Business Innovation. Mega-Corp's award citation reads, 'To Mega-Corp, for the Major Improvements Made to Its Competitive Position Through the Use of Information Systems.' [Notice the use of the past tense—that is, looking back from the future.]

"Imagine that! A presidential award for an information systems strategy! And you all should know that the plans that were implemented during those five years were generated at a single planning meeting—this meeting!

"So I'd like you to stay in the future, imagine the success that Mega-Corp and its divisions have achieved, and 'remember' how these successes were achieved. They required ideas—your ideas— and we would like you to imagine those ideas and write them down, one idea to each Post-it Note. No idea is too small, no idea is silly or stupid, no idea should be edited in your mind. Just let these ideas flow.

"Finally, to make sure we're all on the same track, here is the question that your ideas should be focused on:

[SITUATION SETTING] "It is the year [five years from now]. Mega-Corp has won national and international awards for its information systems contributions to improving corporate competitiveness.

[FUTURE-PULL QUESTION] "How did Mega-Corp use information systems to improve its competitive position?"

Once the Future-Pull question is asked, participants are given 20 to 30 minutes to write as many ideas down as possible. Detail is not requested, only the listing of a large number of ideas. Participants should be politely goaded by the facilitator during this idea-generation phase:

- ○ TIME: "Only 10 minutes left. Make sure all your ideas are expressed."
- ○ NUMBER: "You should have a large number of ideas written down. [Most won't.] Try to double this in the next 10 minutes."
- ○ STRUCTURE: "There are three types of ideas you might think of:
  1. Those you knew when you walked in the door this morning.
  2. Those that occurred to you during the discussion, which you noted on your idea pads.
  3. Those that you are inventing right now, after immersing yourself in the problem."
- ○ INSPIRATION: "Anybody who is not writing down ideas should look at the room's walls. There are many, many sheets mounted describing the various problems and root causes of Mega-Corp's lack of competitive position. Each of those problems should be an inspiration for a new idea, something that can be improved or implemented by information systems. Go through the sheets and write down all the ideas you can think of."

Importance of the Future-Pull Question

In any facilitation, the questions presented by the facilitator are important. In a marketing seminar, they are critical. Remember, "Whatever is asked, the group will answer." Unfortunately, sometimes the wrong question is presented in a facilitation session. In some consulting engagements, the facilitator can go back and

118

rephrase/restart that segment of the discussion. In a seminar situation, however, neither time nor "showmanship" will allow recovery from asking the wrong question.

Notice the difference, for example, between the following two questions:

1. What would your organization gain from information sharing?
2. How would your organization benefit most from information sharing?

The first question asks for a list of potential benefits from information sharing—the capability to share computer-based information easily and quickly. These benefits are important to know, but the question does not produce actionable strategies.

The second question asks almost the same question. What is the difference? With the second question, the expected outcome is a list of *prioritized* benefits—a list that will save time in getting suggested recommendations during a facilitation session. The second question, by asking "how," allows suggestions for how to achieve information sharing in addition to its potential benefits—a result that would not be reached by the first question.

The point should be clear: A facilitator should compose key questions in advance and should review them with the facilitation team or the client. In the case of a marketing seminar, this is especially critical. Facilitators should always plan their questions, test them on others, and try to misinterpret the question intentionally. These efforts will be rewarded by the quality of responses provided in the actual facilitation session.

Creation of Strategies from the Group's Ideas

Once all ideas have been put onto the Post-it Notes, they are gathered in the following way. The facilitator says something like: "Will someone please give me a suggestion that they wrote down? [To cooperative participant: "Thank you."] This idea says, 'Better support for marketing databases.' [First to participant, then to group:] If this idea were part of an idea category, what would that category be?"

Participants will suggest various categories, with the facilitator choosing the best offering or suggesting a new category if no satisfactory suggestions are made. Here a possible category might be "Improved management support for IS"; even better would be "Increased IS participation in competitive strategy."

Then the facilitator continues: "Now that we have an idea category, could everyone please select all their ideas that fit into that category, and give them to me? Thank you."

The ideas are then stuck onto a flipchart page, grouped together, and the category title is put above: "Increased IS Participation in Competitive Strategy." At this point, the facilitator is ready to move on, saying: "Now, could someone provide me with a different idea in a new category, one that is not already on the wall?"

This is done, and done again, until nearly all ideas have been put into categories, mounted, and displayed for all to see. The individual ideas have not been read to the audience, so participants are invited to spend 10 to 15 minutes in a "walking review" of the ideas under each title. During this period, they will see the entire group's creative input and often will see patterns of significance that were not previously apparent. They are also encouraged to put the idea notes into order on each sheet, thereby learning the ideas more thoroughly.

Prioritization of Strategies—Electronic Voting

Meanwhile, the facilitator or cofacilitator has activated the electronic voting system hardware and software. Each of the idea categories, which are now competitive strategies, is entered as a voting topic into the software. Individual ideas are not entered, just the higher-level idea categories.

When the participants have finished their review of the ideas, they use the voting system to indicate which strategies have the greatest future importance for the company. When that vote is complete, they then vote the degree of current performance for all strategies. (Are we currently doing this strategy well or not?)

Interpretation of Voting Map

A resulting Strategic Profile Map Sample is shown in Exhibit 7.1.

The facilitator should then briefly go through the levels of agreement or consensus, by displaying the scatter diagrams for all strategies. Such patterns probably will fall into the patterns shown in Exhibits 7.2, 7.3, and 7.4.

When there is a strategy in the top-left quadrant of the Strategic Profile Map, and that same strategy shows a high degree of consensus, it will be listed among the proposed recommendations of the planning session. Note that in a seminar involving different companies, the degree of consensus will be much lower than in an internal company meeting. Since different companies have different problems, consensus is not to be expected. Nevertheless, the principle of voting consensus should be explained to the audience.

Presentation and Reinforcement of Results to Audience

At this point, the strategic facilitation has produced a fictional "80/20" plan for using information systems to improve Mega-Corp's

Exhibit 7.1   Sample Strategic Map

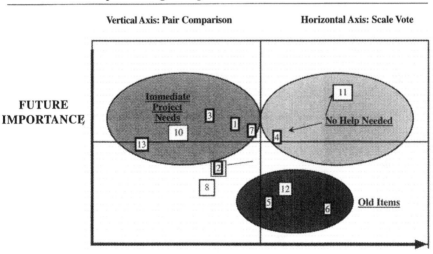

121

Exhibit 7.2   Pattern of Agreement

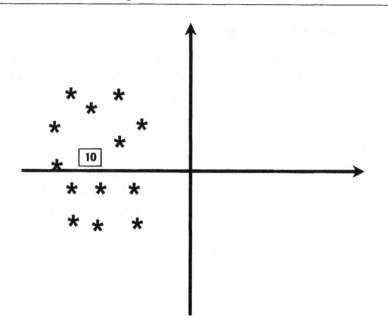

Exhibit 7.3   Disagreement or Confusion

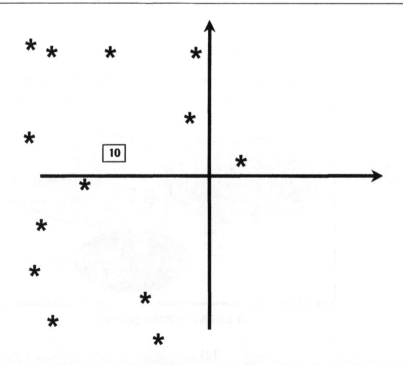

Exhibit 7.4   Pattern of Polarity

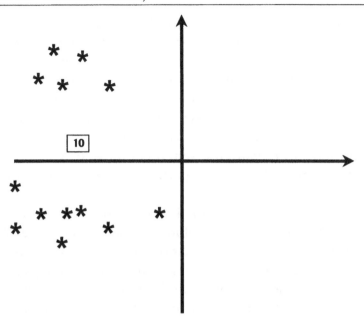

competitive position. There are a number of points to emphasize to the audience:

o The strategies were built entirely from the participants' ideas, not the consultants'.

o It is clear which strategies are favored, through the anonymous voting and the scatter diagrams.

o There are numerous how-to ideas in the groups of Post-it Notes ideas, located under each information strategy.

o This has been only a three-hour demonstration. Actual sessions follow the same process, but take one-to-one-and-a-half days and go into deeper detail. Also, strategic planning sessions can be followed by self-assessment sessions, when they are needed to "fix" a business process.

o Finally, it is clear that the power of facilitated meetings is not simply in obtaining results quickly, but in obtaining consensus and support for the plan from meeting participants.

Stage Presence

A facilitation-based seminar has different requirements of the facilitator than a consulting session. Primary among these is a greater need for "stage presence"—that is, the ability for the facilitator to engage a roomful of participants who do not know each other in a meaningful discussion, to be able to handle different personalities with grace and ease, and to be able to move the facilitation along at an appropriate pace. In some cases, a facilitator also will have to initiate interventions with difficult individuals, but without offending anyone participating in or observing the session.

Stage presence is a personal quality. Some people are born with it, and some learn to develop it. Its applications may range from comedy, to drama, to facilitation, but it is a skill that is essential to bring off a "good show" in a facilitated marketing seminar. Therefore, any facilitator who will be leading a marketing seminar should be well practiced, confident in his or her skills, and able to project those skills and personality to a broad range of participants.

Types of Experience Needed for Facilitation Seminars

Clearly, new facilitators are not expected to take on a facilitated seminar. The risk is too great for a beginner. But how do we choose a facilitator who is capable of leading a facilitated marketing seminar?

The criteria are relatively simple:

o Experience in the facilitation process
o Experience with senior-level executives
o Knowledge and background in the planned subject matter
o An ability to guide participants to the right level of discussion—perspective or "altitude"
o A well-practiced ability to conduct a facilitation in a crisp, well-timed manner

○ The ability to handle difficult issues and/or participants with apparent ease

○ A skill in guiding discussions that will keep participants on the right path, without seeming overbearing or manipulative

These are the key skills. Others may be needed for specific sessions, and should be discussed when choosing a session leader.

Moving from Session, to Report, to Final Proposal

After the facilitation session is over, a written report always should be distributed to participants. For a marketing seminar, the report reinforces the experience of the session and reminds them of the skills of the consulting team. For a single-company client session, the report serves as a written foundation to later consulting proposals and planning sessions. For all types of sessions, a report acts as a positive reinforcement for the session participants, who will see that their time was well spent.

What should be in such a client report? How difficult is it to compose? For the basic facilitation session report, it is a relatively simple task, including:

○ Title page.

○ Executive summary of facilitation session or seminar, presenting the key issues discussed and recommendations made. This will be the ongoing "value statement" of the session and should be written and reviewed with care.

○ Agenda from session.

○ List of participants, with titles (and with company affiliations, if a marketing seminar).

○ List of personal objectives stated at the beginning of the meeting ("self-introductions"), without identification by name.

○ Record of statements made, from handwritten flipchart sheets.

o Voting map(s) showing perceptions of participants.
o Facilitator's interpretation of the voting map(s), including
  – Strategic profile map, showing relative priority of issues.
  – Scatter map, showing degree of consensus or diversity of group on each issue.

This report is not a full consulting report; it is simply a report of a single facilitation session.

The final consulting report, however, is a far more intricate project to write and uses the facilitation session reports as only one form of information input. It is important not to confuse a facilitation session report with a full consulting engagement report.

CONCLUSION

Facilitated seminars often obtain a client sales commitment even before the audience has left the room. This form of marketing seminar frequently pays for itself almost immediately.

A major marketing opportunity exists in facilitation-based seminars. It is up to the reader to be creative with this new facilitative application, to work closely with marketing and sales organizations, and to experiment in making facilitation seminar efforts successful.

8

Different Control Self-Assessment Processes, Different Objectives*

INTRODUCTION

Many professionals start planning for a CSA session by looking at the methodologies used by various consulting firms, large and small. They assume that a single approach—one that will meet all or most of their needs—is out there somewhere. Unfortunately, that is rarely the case.

CSA works best as a style of facilitated consulting, where the facilitator is asking questions focused on achieving a specific outcome. Issues that are common in internal auditing may be tackled with a "precooked" methodology, but CSA tends not to be so cut and dried for its full range of application.

All companies differ in products and services provided, corporate culture, role of internal auditing, or willingness of participants to make time available for CSA sessions. To be fully effective, a CSA

* This first appeared in the September 1998 issue of *CSA Sentinel,* published by The Institute of Internal Auditors. It is reprinted here with permission and minor revisions.

plan needs to reflect all these variables and any others that may obstruct the realization of objectives.

In light of this, it is wise to be wary when consulting firms that are known for a specific CSA methodology suggest that one way is the right way for every organization. From the consultant's standpoint, a single methodology is a useful tool for standardizing services. From the user's standpoint, that one approach may not be optimum in terms of meeting the client's precise needs and concerns. A mismatch can be costly in terms of time, money, and project effectiveness.

POTENTIAL CSA OBJECTIVES AND METHODOLOGIES

A number of variables surface around CSA projects, especially since CSA objectives can be diverse. For example, a CSA might be focused on one or more of the following objectives:

- ○ Determining the key business risks facing an organization
- ○ Determining what is necessary to achieve corporate objectives, where the organization is falling short, and where and how to improve performance
- ○ Examining existing process controls and determining changes to improve their efficiency and effectiveness
- ○ Investigating a business process—anything from shopfloor manufacturing, to accounts payable procedures—to see where it can be improved
- ○ Examining business processes and risks to understand them from multiple perspectives such as employee satisfaction, business risk, or efficiency of operations

Considering the spectrum of applications for CSA encourages most practitioners to adopt a broader perspective for determining where and how CSA fits best in an organization. No single prefabricated consulting methodology can address all of these objectives. Yet CSA, in its broader forms, can and frequently does do so.

From my own experience, I tend to define CSA as a present-tense–oriented facilitation, where questions are presented to clarify issues, determine causation, and reach potential solutions. Having a broad and flexible definition can be helpful in escaping the fixed methodology trap that has pervaded the field of internal audit consultation.

Determining Key Business Risks

A number of key stakeholders are gathered for a four- to six-hour CSA discussion. Interviewing may or may not have been conducted beforehand, but the session has been precisely planned to cover the entire subject matter thoroughly. These preparations focus on defining the subject matter to be discussed, breaking it into smaller and more manageable segments, and preparing questions in advance.

Typically, a fixed format of questions are asked within one-hour segments of discussion. The series of questions might include:

○ How does this business process operate?
○ Where is it successful? What examples reveal this?
○ Specifically, where are there problems in this business process? What might prevent it achieving its objectives?
○ What suggestions are there to improve the situation?

A list of business risks is extracted from the answers to the third question, across all discussion segments, which is then prioritized using an anonymous voting system. The resulting maps show clearly what the key risks are, which are most threatening, and which risks have the greatest exposure for the enterprise.

Helping to Achieve Corporate Objectives

Under one methodology, the MAPCO approach, a key corporate objective is broken down into 10 to 12 supporting objectives. Each supporting objective is then measured through voting. Participants submit votes, on a scale of 1 to 7, on both the actual and desired effectiveness of each supporting objective. The gap between actual and desired effectiveness shows how great the performance shortfall is—thus generating a priority scale for assigning resources in the audit plan. Each supporting objective is then discussed to elicit comments on its inherent "successes" and "obstacles." At the end, recommendations are recorded, but only if agreed upon by all participants.

Examining Existing Process Controls

Examining existing process controls helps determine where changes are needed in the control process. This approach, developed by Tim Leech of MCS Consulting, focuses closely on the controls in place and asks a series of questions, such as:

○ What is the risk?
○ What are the controls?
○ What is the gap between them? Is it acceptable?
○ Is the "control portfolio" optimized; that is, are there cost efficiencies to be gained?

There are both advantages and disadvantages to this process. The basic advantage is that this is an excellent approach for a departmental examination of existing process controls, since it asks clear questions about a known subject. The Leech approach has gained much popularity because of this, and is often mentioned as a method for stakeholders to design their own process controls.

The disadvantage is that these questions are often too narrowly focused to give true managerial value. This approach deals with controls from "inside" the process, while other "outside view" approaches are more suitable to examinations of business risk. The higher-level view of management demands that open-ended questions be asked (e.g., "Where is the risk to our business?"). Also, the involvement of all levels of departmental personnel prevents discussion of more abstract and cross-departmental issues.

Investigating a Business Process

Investigating a business process is a complex CSA objective, in which discussion can be organized along vertical, horizontal, or diagonal dimensions.

- Vertical discussion requires looking at a single department/process from top to bottom, involving all levels of employees related to the business process in question.
- Horizontal discussion assesses the process or problem across the entire enterprise but at a specific level of management—examining and comparing where problems arise, what their common causes might be, and how these problems might be solved.
- Diagonal discussion calls for taking a cross-organizational situation and studying it in any way required. This type of assessment often requires a sampling approach via numerous CSA sessions across geographies, management levels, and operational processes. Such an approach might be used, for example, in raising the level of product quality across all manufacturing operations.

Typically, the process flow is diagrammed into a series of high-level charts. Then each chart, representing a major subprocess, is described to the group and discussed in detail. Discussion might be based on questions similar to those listed in the first objective. Once all information from the questions has been complied, it is closely assessed to determine where possible improvements can be made.

Examining Processes and Risks from Multiple Perspectives

Examining processes and risks from multiple perspectives requires a multidimensional discussion on business risk. For example, a manufacturing company might conduct CSA sessions to improve operational quality. The dimensions of "quality" in this CSA approach might include efficiency, effectiveness, accuracy of production, performance to cost budget, performance to time budget, flexibility in product redesign, and customer satisfaction with finished product.

YOUR OWN CONTROL SELF-ASSESSMENT

Evaluating this range of objectives will help facilitators tailor objectives specifically to an organization's needs, thus taking advantage of the fluidity of CSA. The diversity of these CSA objectives is met with a whole arsenal of prefabricated methodologies and approaches. No single CSA process has been constructed, however, to meet the universal needs of every organization.

CSA is a process for group discussion that elicits facts, causation, and potential solutions using almost any discussion approach that the mind can envision. If you can imagine researching an issue through one-on-one individual management interviews, you are probably two-thirds of the way toward defining an effective CSA methodology for an organization. Then issues of group interaction, formalizing the questions into a usable script, setting up electronic voting, and other CSA tools and techniques can be addressed.

If an outside consulting firm says it has a world-class CSA methodology that precisely fits your problem, think twice. As the client, you should be integrally involved in the development or customizing of an *appropriate* CSA methodology. If the CSA process feels comfortable to you, it is probably appropriate to the subject matter and vice versa. Your problems deserve fresh thinking and fresh approaches—in other words, a CSA engagement methodology designed to fit your needs.

CASE STUDY: A MULTI–CONTROL SELF-ASSESSMENT ENGAGEMENT

CSA can take on many forms and *should* do so for maximum effectiveness. Below is a sample of a multi-CSA engagement that adopted this approach. The engagement required meeting several desired objectives in order to reach its eventual goal: a unified, statewide audit plan. Although only two major CSA processes are presented here, the principle stands out that no single CSA methodology is right for all purposes.

Multiple Objectives

A state government hired outside consultants to develop a statewide audit plan. It was requested that CSA be utilized within the consulting process. For this audit plan, CSA performed two key roles:

1. Determining the key business risks selected and voted on by the control administrators of all state agencies.
2. Determining whether the business process flow diagrams developed by the engagement team were complete, accurate, and reflective of the way the government agencies operate.

Votes also were taken at the beginning of each facilitation meeting to determine which risk categories should be considered high priority or low priority when assigning audit resources.

Key Business Risks

The first project called for presession interviews to be conducted with all participants. Each participant was asked an identical script of questions, including a request to name the top five risks facing the state government. The resulting list included 89 business risks across four major transaction cycles.

Despite this high number of business risks, accurate and consistent voting results were achieved. Mathematical rankings were derived according to risk magnitude, threat of risk, and postcontrol exposure. Often the same items scored high in all areas: magnitude, threat, and exposure. This demonstrated a high consistency of data, increasing the significance of the votes.

Accuracy of Process Flow Diagrams

Extensive effort was invested in developing high-level process flow diagrams—one for each major transaction cycle within the state government. Subsequently, the key question asked whether these flow diagrams were complete and accurate. A customized CSA methodology was developed to answer that question, which validated the flow diagrams for use in the statewide audit plan.

The CSA methodology used here was organized as follows:

- o All process flow diagrams were drawn up using a similar perspective, or "altitude," that was sufficiently high to be understandable yet still provided an accurate description of the business process.
- o Each consultant acted as "process flow expert" for the diagrams that were developed. As a result, all consultants presented the diagrams directly to the management group and fielded all questions.
- o The facilitator's role involved introducing the process flow expert and asking whether the process diagram was both accurate and complete after it had been described. The facilitator also assisted in motivating the subsequent discussion, spotting areas of disagreement or lack of understanding, bringing ideas into the open, and helping clarify the issues.
- o Once the process flow diagram was completed, the CSA process was repeated with the introduction of the next diagram and expert.

The data acquired from this CSA process then was used to identify the most effective audit controls and assign appropriate resources in the final audit plan. As a result, this multi-CSA successfully developed a statewide, full-year audit plan, which is currently being implemented.

9

Necessary Skills, Qualities, and Values of a Facilitator

INTRODUCTION

For many business professionals, the art of facilitation does not come naturally; and for others, it requires little to no training. This chapter will set forth the skills, qualities, and values that will help a person succeed in a facilitation effort. It will also provide good review material for those who have a natural facilitation capacity but may never have had formal training.

BASIC VALUES OF FACILITATION

Asking, Not Telling

The most important concept for new facilitators is their role to ask, not tell. In the group leadership role, adopting a "tell" personality will establish the facilitator as a content leader or a subject-matter expert. Even worse from the facilitation viewpoint, it may establish (or reinforce) the facilitator as a political leader of the group. In any of these cases, the group will look to the facilitator for guidance in voicing their opinions, in citing situations or facts to support different perspectives, or even in choosing actions to pursue. This is the opposite of the facilitator's desired role, for two reasons:

1. Facilitation is a process skill, enabling facilitators to lead discussions with only a minimal expertise in the particular subject matter. Once their role transitions to subject-matter expert, they are limited in the range of sessions they can lead. Once the role of process expert is mastered, however, successful facilitators can lead a surprisingly wide range of meetings.

2. Once participants start to view the facilitator as a leader of the group's interaction, they will "take a backseat" and wait for that leadership to be exerted. Even worse, if the facilitator exerts political force in predetermining a particular outcome of the meeting or in forcing a particular perspective of the facts, the group will resent this intrusion and stop or limit their free participation in the discussions.

The facilitator's role is dependent on the participants' trust. Once that trust is lost, it is impossible to ever recover it fully. Moreover, it is that trust which gives participants the "space" to offer individual opinions, unpopular views, unexpected facts—exactly the content that gives facilitated meetings their extraordinary effectiveness.

When acting as facilitator, you must adopt a neutral, nonjudgmental attitude toward the meeting and its output. Except for an enthusiastic, positive, and results-oriented style, questions and comments should be delivered without personal involvement in the response. The applications of this approach are effective in gathering facts, in eliciting opinions, and in moving the group toward action-oriented ideas. As you advance in your facilitation experience, you will find that offering any opinion will change your relationship with the group, no matter how good it has been. It may not instantly turn into a poor relationship, but many participants will be more careful about what they say. The reason for this is they now see you as another participant, not just an "encourager." This means that you may be judging them rather than playing the true facilitator role—helping the group suspend judgment to encourage participation.

Therefore, remember that the group's success in your meeting will depend on the quantity and quality of their participation. When a facilitator acts as a process expert, not a content expert, that participation is encouraged. Therefore, remember that a true facilitator always is in an asking mode, not a telling mode.

As an example, remember that the facilitator's most frequent question will be "What else?"—a question that encourages all members of the group to contribute more and more information. When no one has a response to "What else?" the group's information has been drained, and the discussion can move on.

Gaining Consensus

First, it is necessary to define "consensus." In earlier times, consensus meant full unanimity among a group. This is not realistic to expect, and, in fact, expecting it hinders the effectiveness of any group discussion. In the latter half of the twentieth century, however, a new meaning for consensus developed: the concept of "political consensus," or sufficient agreement for the group to move ahead with a decision. This is the definition that operates in a facilitative environment: not that all members of the group should agree that a particular answer is correct, but that disagreeing members understand the perspective of the others and are willing to accept it. (For example, the following definition is provided in *The American Heritage Dictionary*, 2nd College Edition: "Consensus – 1. Collective opinion: *The workers' consensus was that the tax bill was a good one*. 2. General agreement or accord.")

Facilitators sometimes will find that older participants are not familiar with this use of the word. In those cases it is recommended that the term be formally defined at the start of the meeting. This will help establish a more cooperative approach, since there is no pressure for unanimity.

Patience Brings Far Better Results

A second aspect of gaining agreement is to understand that it will come from the group's own development of ideas, not from the facilitator's direction. Apart from asking questions that will develop understanding of the varied perspectives, the facilitator can do little to make a group develop the necessary consensus to adopt ideas or plan activities. Therefore, it is critical that the facilitator understand the need for patience and positivity: Far more can be gained by asking "What are the differences in these perspectives?" than in suggesting "Let's select an approach to pursue."

The major exception to the facilitator's neutrality in selecting options to pursue is the use of electronic, anonymous voting systems. These computer-based tools allow participants to vote their own preferences without fear of group reaction, and to see the group's reactions without knowing how individuals voted. This has a powerful effect in a facilitated meeting: After hours of developing ideas and distilling them into possible action strategies, it provides a neutral, factual basis for choosing among alternative possibilities. Note, however, that the voting results are not the meeting's recommendations in themselves: The participants must see those results, understand them, and then formally decide to accept whichever strategies are appropriate.

More detailed information on electronic voting systems is provided in Chapter 10, including exhibits of voting system output maps.

Nearly All Information Can Be Valuable

Most facilitators, early in their careers, try to keep the discussion on point by limiting the range of comments from the meeting's participants. Even the first time that this happens, it has a chilling effect on the rest of the meeting. Participants sense that there are comments that will be approved and others that will be disapproved. From a meeting dynamics perspective, it is the wrong approach.

From a content perspective, however, limiting the range of comments is even more deleterious. Most situations under discussion in a facilitated meeting have been under consideration in other settings. Often the facilitation is being held because the results of those other discussions were not sufficient to achieve the organization's goals. They may have failed in defining a plan of action, in getting to a sufficient level of detail, or in any number of other ways. Therefore, participants and management expect that the facilitated approach, which requires a significant time investment from participants, will achieve better results. Limiting the range of participant comments will hinder achieving these goals. In fact, unusual or outside-the-box thinking often will lead to a fresh perspective on the situation, frequently enabling the group to solve its unique situation in a unique way.

Finally, often an the unusual perspective or generally unknown fact opens the door for creating new ideas and new plans, or for exposing prior reasons for disagreement. With new facts, old disagreements can often be ended, either because the facts themselves do not support the disagreement or because the new facts give a basis (even just a "face-saving" basis) for changing participants' prior rigid positions.

Therefore, a facilitator should always keep an open mind and should never be judgmental. Encouraging participation is an important guiding principle in all facilitated discussions.

Seeing Patterns of Discussion and Behavior

A facilitator's role is to be a discussion *leader*. The word "leader" has many meanings and requires many different skills. One of the most important is the ability to be "above the discussion" and see the developing patterns of participant comments. Once having seen these patterns, the facilitator can help the group by encouraging further thinking along paths that lead to successful outcomes, bypassing random or nonproductive paths. Although this process could be characterized as manipulative, it is an essential role for the facilitator to play. Without such assistance, the session would be no more productive than other, nonstructured meetings.

Note that this principle is different from the concept of keeping comments at the correct level—overseeing the appropriate specificity or perspective of comments. This issue will be discussed later under "Leading a Focused Discussion."

MEETING LEADERSHIP

Understanding Group Dynamics

For an experienced facilitator, there are constant observations of the meeting occurring during the course of the session. Many are devoted to the immediate discussion:

- ○ Is the comment helpful to the discussion?
- ○ Is there a negative purpose to the comment, which could sidetrack the meeting?
- ○ Is the group being attentive?

Simultaneously, the facilitator is focusing on other, longer-range issues:

- ○ Is the discussion proceeding toward achieving its stated goals?
- ○ Is the group tending to converge or agree more in the discussions, or to diverge?
- ○ Will the meeting reach its goals within the time allocated?
- ○ Is the process specified for the meeting succeeding? Are changes needed?

A few of the major issues to understand are set forth below.

When to Push versus Pull. Traditional management theories typically focused on the forceful or dominant qualities of the managerial personality:

- ○ Establishing authority
- ○ Having command of situations
- ○ Getting directives followed

Surprisingly, all these principles are harmful to a facilitation session and to a facilitator's development as a skilled professional. The basic reasons are set forth under "Basic Values of Facilitation." However, it is not enough to understand what is harmful; you also must know what is the desired behavior to exercise.

The answer to this problem is to consider the difference between "push" and "pull" psychological approaches. All of the above traditional principles involve forceful, push-type behaviors. To succeed in any of them, one projects personal power in a directive way. Facilitative leadership, however, can be better accomplished when one exerts a force that draws out other people. In this approach, a well-timed question ("Do we all agree on this strategy?") will have far better results than a forceful statement ("Let's move ahead with this.").

The facilitator's role, therefore, is to use the "pull philosophy" to its utmost degree:

o Always ask leading questions.
o Often state positive suggestions, but not so strongly as to direct the outcome—just enough to open new paths of thought.
o Regarding when to push versus pull, the answer is clear: Always focus on the pull facilitative style. Never, or hardly ever, push participants individually or as a group.

When Interventions Are Needed. As people become more fully involved in the facilitative art, it soon becomes clear that they are swimming in a psychological ocean. Meetings are far more than content statements; they consist of individual and group feelings, reactions, and dynamics.

Once that is understood, it is a simple step to realize the potential for negative interpersonal activities, communications, and dynamics. A facilitated meeting is frequently an open platform for voicing all types of opinions. Such meetings will often uncover negative attitudes, interpersonal difficulties, and attempts to dominate the meeting's outcome.

Are Objectives Being Achieved? Facilitation can be a "soft art" that simply helps participants talk, feel good, and "get it out." Those are not business goals, and *business* facilitation always must achieve specific objectives. Therefore, it is up to the facilitator to ensure that those objectives are being met.

How is this done? By constant listening, understanding, seeing the patterns of conversation, and sensing whether they are constructive in terms of addressing the specific issues of the meeting. The facilitator is, in some ways, the representative of the meeting's sponsors. They have set aside critical resources (the participants and their time away from work) to achieve a goal. It is up to the facilitator to ensure that that investment is well managed. This is not to say that the facilitator represents management's views. To do so would destroy their credibility and leadership and would greatly lower the quality of the meeting.

Is the Meeting Process Successful?   For different meetings and different objectives, a skilled facilitator will select different facilitation processes or modify traditional ones to fit the client's needs. Once the best process has been chosen or designed, an agenda is created to fit the underlying process structure. (More about this subject appears in Chapter 8.)

Choosing a process and designing an agenda do not, however, fulfill the facilitator's responsibilities. He or she also must monitor the meeting at a high perspective, observing whether the meeting's process is, in fact, successful. If it is, the facilitator's role is simplified by one dimension. If it is not, the facilitator must see the problem in its early stages and try to remedy the defect by managing the existing process more tightly. The goal is to focus better on achieving stated objectives or, if necessary, doing a midcourse correction and modifying the facilitation process.

Modifying the meeting's underlying process should be considered only as a last resort. Not only will a new approach have significantly less time to succeed, given that the original meeting already has been under way, but the change of format will be profoundly disturbing to participants. When the meeting was started, participants were expecting a certain format—perhaps inferred from the agenda, perhaps openly described by the facilitator at the start of the session. In either event, by this time participants will understand "the rhythm" of the meeting and will be upset by major changes. Changing the meeting process during a session should, therefore, be reserved for the most extreme circumstances.

How, then, can a facilitator alter the course of an unsuccessful meeting? Often this can be done by halting the discussion, "opening up" to the group about the difficulties being observed, and asking for their suggestions and assistance. Once asked to help in redirecting an unsuccessful meeting, many participants will pitch in to help bring the session back on track.

Are We on Time? As simple as it may sound, keeping the meeting on time is one of the facilitator's most difficult tasks. It requires constant observation of the meeting's progress at a level higher than all others. Whether the conversation is on track, objectives are being achieved, or interventions are needed are inputs to the on-time equation.

The facilitator should be keeping another high-level observation in mind during the entire progress of the session. It is common for beginning facilitators to allow excessive time for discussions at the start of the meeting, causing them to speed up discussions in its final stages. This is a mistake, since the ending discussions are the time when agreements are formed and action plans are set. Therefore, it is critical for the facilitator to allocate time appropriately in setting the agenda and to keep to that timing throughout the session.

FACILITATOR'S MIND-SET

In addition to values and techniques, it is also important to consider the necessary mind-set for success in conducting facilitations. By mind-set we mean the necessary internal attitudes and perspectives that will help a facilitator achieve success. In many cases, the right attitude will mean the difference between success and failure, both in handling the situation correctly and in being perceived positively by the participant group.

Commitment to Participants

Commitment to participants is by far the most important of all the attitudes leading to facilitator success. Not only does this convey a positive image to the participants, it is also the facilitator's deepest resource when difficulties are encountered during the session. The depth of this commitment will determine whether a facilitator can come up with the right solutions, communicate them effectively, and bring the participant group through their difficulties.

The facilitator must have a deep and sincere commitment to the participants and to assisting them in meeting their objectives. In many senses, the facilitator is a sole actor on an empty stage. If the play is to succeed, it will be due to the facilitator's ability. Therefore, when difficulties arise, a facilitator must understand this principle and accept responsibility for the meeting's success. Understanding and accepting that responsibility, together with an internal dedication to help participants fulfill their needs, frequently will make internal resources more available to a facilitator. These resources, nearly visceral in their depth, are what count in delivering the highest-quality sessions.

Neutrality

Facilitations frequently involve serious and complex issues. Simpler matters are typically decided through traditional management processes, and it is the hard ones that get to the facilitative stage. Like any human being, a facilitator will tend to form opinions on the issues as the discussions progress. Forming these opinions is human and unavoidable. Letting them influence the conduct of the session cannot be allowed. Once the facilitator is seen to have opinions and therefore is likely to push for a particular outcome, the essential credibility of the facilitative process is lost. Participants will immediately sense, or perhaps fear, manipulation of the meeting to fulfill the facilitator's opinions. Whether that is the case or not, the participants' perceptions determine whether the meeting can succeed. The only answer is for the facilitator to keep a neutral perspective as much as possible.

The question of manipulation, however, has both positive and negative aspects. While facilitators cannot allow their opinions to shape the conversation, they constantly must influence the course of the meeting to keep it on track. Although both activities could be considered manipulation, using influence to minimize off-track comments and keep the discussion moving in desired directions is a positive purpose. The difference can be subtle in some situations, and it is up to the facilitator's own conscience as to which principle applies.

Facilitator Involvement

A corollary issue to meeting manipulation is facilitator involvement. In general, it is desirable for a facilitator to be emotionally involved in a session, but not if it leads the facilitator to misguide the meeting or to influence it toward one outcome or another.

The positive aspects of emotional involvement are those that bring the facilitator into alignment with the meeting objectives and to helping the participants reach their best outcome. This is an opportunity for positive meeting leadership as well as developing a close relationship with participants, both being useful and productive in guiding the session.

Guidance, Support: YES. The facilitator's true role is to act as the participants' guide and helper, focused toward the goal of achieving the meeting's objectives. Therefore, the successful facilitator will maximize all guiding and supporting behaviors while remaining neutral regarding specific perspectives, decisions, or outcomes.

Most frequently, this guidance and support will be expressed through skillful group leadership, as opposed to statements of "Let me help here." Also, the facilitator should be sure not to lecture, but to guide and support through effective application of facilitative techniques. The key to understanding the difference is to realize that the group does not relate to the facilitator in a personal way. Rather, they see a facilitator as a neutral force that exerts necessary influence through meeting leadership and generally not through comments directed person to person.

For example, if two participants exhibited hostility, a facilitator might take two different approaches:

- *Personal/Discouraged:* "Jim, please tone down your comments. And Jane, I would appreciate your doing that too."
- *Neutral Leadership/Encouraged:* (Stepping between the participants in a U-shape table arrangement or beside them if U-shape not available. Facilitator looks at any participants other than the two exhibiting hostility.) "What might be the basis for these two viewpoints? Are they exclusive? Must we choose between them? Or can we bring about some sort of balanced solution?"

Emotions? Content? No. It does not matter how a facilitator feels. Period. The facilitator's job is not to become emotionally involved, not to allow emotional reactions internally or to exhibit them externally. The facilitator must rise above personal reactions, since they will only lessen the quality of a session.

Similarly, it does not matter what a facilitator thinks. Period. Just like emotional involvement, the facilitator should disregard personal knowledge of the subject matter during the session. A facilitator should use this knowledge only to construct effective questions and understand the meeting's progress. At no time can a facilitator risk losing the group's acceptance by offering a fact, an opinion, or an experience. Surprisingly, this principle applies just as much to contributing content that is neutral and helpful as it does to facts that only support one side of a debate. Once a facilitator acts as a content expert, the group's perception is permanently changed. The facilitator will have a difficult time regaining the group's acceptance.

Patience Required at All Times

As in all things, patience is a virtue. But when a facilitator is at the beginning of a six-hour, one-day, or even three-day session, it is a requirement. In many sessions, the issues are contentious and the participants can be difficult. The facilitator needs to remain steadfast and not be discouraged. More important, the facilitator must learn to trust the process. With a properly designed meeting and reasonable facilitative skills, nearly all contentious situations will defuse as the meeting progresses. Having confidence in the facilitative process will make it easier for new facilitators to be patient in dealing with difficult issues or clients.

The facilitator also needs to exhibit patience to the participant group. If a facilitator seems impatient and unable to deal emotionally with issues, the quality of the session will deteriorate quickly. No matter how difficult the issue, the facilitator must remain neutral, effective, and patient.

The Facilitator As "Servant of the Group"

Some of the principles set forth in this chapter may seem lofty and unattainable. To assist the new facilitator in keeping to these principles, a few intentionally adopted attitudes may be helpful:

- Facilitators should see themselves as servants of the group.
- A facilitator's influence on the meeting (i.e., when comments are getting off-track) should be exercised through well-formed, leading questions. It is never effective to dictate to the group.
- The facilitator should be listening to the group's comments in a "leading mode"; that is, understanding the comments themselves and also seeing in what direction the comments will lead the conversation. When discussion is off-course, thoughtful questions can redirect the meeting. When specific comments and the general discussion are on-course, the facilitator may well choose to let the discussion continue without intervention.
- The facilitator often can lead a well-focused discussion merely by keeping it at the right pace. When comments slow down, simple leading questions can be used (e.g., "What else do we know about this issue?" or "Are there any other comments?").
- Facilitators' credibility will be seriously threatened if they are seen as favoring one side of the discussion or the other, or one individual over another. Therefore, facilitators should

not voice disapproval or disagreement with a participant. The converse case, however, is just as important: Facilitators should not approve or agree with a single viewpoint or a single individual. Once approval is expressed, the lack of explicit statements of approval will be perceived as statements of disapproval. Therefore, true neutrality requires both nonapproval and nondisapproval.

o At every stage of the session, facilitators should be asking questions and exerting influence in a way that tends to build consensus. Here there are two issues to remember: Questions must be both positively oriented and phrased in positive ways. For example, when seeking to establish agreement on an issue (the positive orientation), the facilitative question would be "Are we agreed on this?" rather than "Does anybody disagree?" The first question will bring head nods and positive indications of consensus; the second question will highlight the disagreement in the room. In the long run, major consensus is built on a foundation of smaller agreements, and the form of a facilitator's questions will help this process along.

BROADENING THE COMFORT ZONE

When difficult issues are under examination, the normal tendency is for groups to stay within their comfort zone. Typically, most participants will tend not to voice disagreement in a public forum, yet no facilitation can be effective unless those disagreements are stated. The challenge is to ensure that they are voiced without leading to hostility among the group, and this means taking the participants beyond their normal business-meeting behavior.

Three psychological zones are depicted in Exhibit 9.1:

1. The comfort zone, where participants are willing to contribute a limited range of information.
2. The discomfort zone, where a broader range of information is provided but it is uncomfortable for the participants.

Exhibit 9.1   Comfort Zone

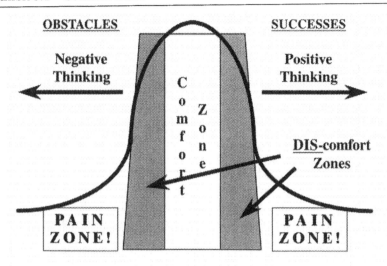

3. The pain zone, where a full range of information is available but where extreme discomfort or psychological pain can be caused by in the most extreme statements or contributions (e.g., where participants are asked to reveal negative experiences with high emotional impact).

Here the facilitator's goal is to move the discussion outside the comfort zone yet not so far as the pain zone. A facilitation is not a group encounter; it is a business discussion. While contributions in the discomfort zone are recommended, comments in the pain zone range are not. Why? First, the facilitator does not have the client's, the group's, or the individual's permission to demand information that can be painful. Second, the effect of the emotional pain may affect both that individual's and the group's willingness to continue their contributions to the discussion.

MANAGING THE EMOTIONS OF THE GROUP

While facilitators should keep a tight rein on their own emotions and exhibit neutrality, different principles are involved in dealing with the emotions of the group and of individuals within the group. These six principles are as follows:

1. Most participant emotions are good and constructive, and the facilitator's role is to harness them to achieve the group's objectives. Energy, motivation, commitment, and a desire for action are all positive emotions, and a skilled facilitator will use them to elicit positive suggestions and to generate group consensus.

2. Some negative emotions can be good and also can be harnessed. Examples include participant disagreements with each other that are based on factual knowledge or differing perspectives. Frequently these comments will serve to broaden the viewpoints of the group as a whole and will serve as the first step to creating solutions that can be accepted by all. Other disagreements could be meant constructively, as when a participant might comment that the facilitator's questions are not on target. Here the intent is to improve the meeting.

3. When faced with disagreement, the facilitator's first reaction should be to inquire neutrally as to the basis for the disagreement. In no event should the facilitator be drawn into an argument on the disagreed-upon issue. The purpose of the facilitator's role is simply to help participants understand the basis of their disagreement so that they can develop an agreed-upon approach. Frequently this can be achieved by asking simple, open-ended questions that provide "space" for group members to participate. Tightly focused questions (e.g., "Why do you feel that way?"), however, can inhibit participation.

4. When participants disagree for positive reasons and a spirited (but well-intentioned) discussion ensues, the facilitator generally should stay out of the discussion. In most cases, participants will discover the basis of their disagreement and move on to developing consensus positions. Here the

facilitator can assist by asking constructive questions and should not be tempted to cut off conversation merely because there are opposing sides.

5. The underlying force in a facilitative meeting is having a shared objective. This is typically stated at the beginning of a session for the group to consider and accept or in some cases to modify and accept. Once the shared objective is accepted, it is a foundation for the entire session. Disagreements are constructive when both or all sides of the discussions still remain within the shared objective. Divisive discussions generally result when there is no shared objective, when it has been insufficiently impressed upon the group at the beginning of the meeting, or when a single individual is trying to dominate the group. (The last is, of course, an excellent example of a nonshared objective.) In general, facilitators should encourage participation by all and, in particular, by more introverted members of the group; in particular, they should prevent extroverts or senior managers from dominating the session.

6. As a general rule, facilitators will be able to deal with disagreements better when they follow the rule "Facilitators should check their egos at the door."

DIFFICULT BEHAVIORS BY PARTICIPANTS

Often behaviors shown in facilitation sessions need to be understood and managed. Usually they do not threaten the success of the meeting, but are just the natural result of any group interaction. Facilitators are asked simply to be aware of them and prepared for their appearance during sessions. (For more severe situations, see "Meeting Interventions" later in this chapter.)

Some of these behaviors include:

○ **Domination of the meeting or of other participants.** Participant tries to act as facilitator to achieve his or her own purposes, or psychologically tries to control other participants.

o **Lazy attitudes.** Whining, complaining, or other similar behaviors.

o **Obstructive attitudes.** Constant disagreement without factual basis.

o **Last-Word Disorder.** A frequent symptom of domination, where the participant refuses to compromise and browbeats others through endless responses.

o **Management insecurity.** Exhibited by interfering with free and open discussion, seeing it as a threat to authority.

UNDERSTANDING AND MANAGING CONFLICT IN THE MEETING

Conflict in a meeting can be divided into positive and negative conflict.

Positive conflict can be defined as conflict derived from the session subject matter, where discussion of the difficulty can advance the group's understanding and help achieve consensus. The principles of managing positive conflict were described under "Managing the Emotions of the Group" earlier in this chapter.

Negative conflict can be defined as conflict that hinders or prevents achieving the outcome(s) of the workshop. The following are principles for managing negative conflicts and behaviors that may occur during a session:

o Set ground rules in advance and reinforce them to the participants as necessary. Sample ground rules are set forth in Exhibit 9.2.

o "Step on" or discourage the first negative personal comments that are made, typically with a mild rebuke. (For example, "Let's remember the ground rules. Personal comments are not part of this meeting.") When negative personal comments are made, they are always destructive to the atmosphere of a facilitation session. Therefore, they should be dealt with immediately. Putting off or avoiding this will lead to the same person repeating the behavior or to others copying it with negative effect on the meeting. Nevertheless, the facilitator will need to find constructive ways to stop these comments.

o Listen for a potential contribution to the subject. What may seem to be negative conflict may simply be a positive disagreement expressed poorly.

o Reframe milder comments into constructive terms. One of the key skills for a facilitator is to be able to rephrase—in this case, turning a negative comment into a positive question.

o Ask the group for their reaction to the content of the comment. (Facilitators should focus on the process and psychological side of the meeting, leaving content judgments to participants.) In some cases, it will be helpful to encourage participants by stating the content of the remark, ignoring its style or phrasing.

o If high emotions and emotional comments continue, ask the speaker for reasons for the "strength of feelings." In this way, a charged comment can become a revealing conversation. If this does not help, move on to the "Meeting Interventions" section of this chapter.

o Allow the discussion to continue if there is valuable input. Try to separate the comment's negative emotion from its core content: Just because there is disagreement, the comment should not be ignored.

o Put a higher perspective on the comment(s): Summarize the discussion in a constructive framework. For example, if executive participants dismiss the disagreements of a lower-level worker, ask: "Is it possible that this is a more realistic view of this process? Do we have facts to say that his/her disagreement was wrong?"

Exhibit 9.2 Sample Ground Rules

- Participants should focus on the discussion and be supportive and constructive in their comments.

- Participants are asked to keep on schedule.

- No personal criticisms or comments are allowed.

- This meeting is private and confidential. Beyond matters to be reported publicly, all comments should be kept confidential.

- Please turn off pagers and cell phones; no messages.

- Breaks have been provided for messages and calls.

SETTING GROUND RULES

It is far easier for a facilitator to manage a difficult group if ground rules have been established first. Rather than have to "make it up as you go along," the facilitator simply can refer to the ground rules that were announced at the start of the meeting (and implicitly accepted by the participants). Groups experienced in facilitation sessions may not need these; beginning groups will. Exhibit 9.2 shows a sample set of ground rules.

USE OF HUMOR

Unless one is an accomplished comedian with a low-key style, it is difficult to make humor an effective tool for facilitation. Different types of humor are described next, together with their particular areas of difficulty.

○ **Gentle Humor.** This is the only style of humor that has a reasonable chance of success in facilitating a group session. It can help create a relaxed feeling in the group, perhaps restarting a discussion that has halted. It also helps the group see the facilitator as more human rather than robotic. Finally, it can help calm troubled waters or revive a boring discussion.

○ **Silly Humor.** This type of humor can make the facilitator appear immature and will certainly lower the group's respect for them and the role they are playing.

○ **Crazy Humor.** This is a high-risk approach to humor, with rare success. It is not appropriate for CSA sessions, due to their businesslike approach to analyzing business processes and risks. On the other hand, it may be appropriate in a strategic planning session where new ideas and out-of-the-box thinking is encouraged—sometimes a joke with an unusual perspective can suggest new ideas.

○ **Personal/Destructive Humor.** *Never* use this type of humor, whether directed at an individual or a group (ethnic, religious, etc.). No matter how harmless the intention, it always will reflect badly on the facilitator and usually will be taken as insulting. Even a single instance of personal/destructive humor can seriously threaten the success of a meeting.

MEETING INTERVENTIONS

No individual is perfect, and the same rule applies to groups. Facilitators often encounter behaviors that are annoying to others, that interfere with the group's progress, or that are clearly damaging to the session. There are specific techniques for dealing with them, ranging from minor interventions to overt challenge of the interfering party. Exhibit 9.3 provides a list of these interventions.

Notice that the interventions in the exhibit are both numbered and grouped. The numbering is in the sequence order of their use. The #1 intervention should be tried first; if it is ineffective, the #2 intervention used; and so on. The interventions are placed into two groups:

1. *Win-Win:* Use of these interventions, if effective, will not hurt the atmosphere of the session or the progress being

Exhibit 9.3   Meeting Interventions

START

WIN-WIN:
1. **Make eye contact briefly.**
2. **Walk halfway to them (outside their bubble).**
3. **Stand beside, face group (invade bubble).**
4. **Quote ground rules while looking directly at them.**

WIN-LOSE:
5. **Ask them a question.**
6. **Make polite, direct hand gesture to them.**
7. **Talk and/or touch directly.**
8. **Confront at break.**
9. **Confront openly in front of group.**

END

made. This is because the interaction with the problem participant does not make him or her "lose face" before the other participants. In fact, effective use of Win-Win interventions may not even be noticed.

2. *Win-Lose:* Use of these interventions sets up a challenge between the facilitator and the problem participant. For the sake of the meeting, the facilitator must win; for the sake of his or her ego, the participant must win. Therefore, there will be a loss of face for the participant if the

meeting is to go on. The degree of the loss of face, or even humiliation, increases at each step of the win-lose intervention. Therefore facilitators should be cautious in using these techniques.

Interventions #2 and #3 mention the participants' "bubbles" of space. Every person requires a certain space around themselves, empty of others' presence, to feel secure. For many people, this is about a three-foot radius; however, it will increase with feelings of insecurity and anger and will decrease with feelings of security and closeness. Intentionally, but gently, invading this bubble will slightly startle a participant and will definitely get his or her attention, even if the person is not aware of the concept of bubbles.

Also, please note that intervention #7 ("Talk and/or Touch Directly") should be followed cautiously regarding touching. The suggested method is to lightly touch the person's hand on a desk in front of the facilitator, or perhaps place a hand lightly on the shoulder of a person sitting beside the facilitator. Touching should be taken no further than that, and even that level of touch should be considered carefully in advance; some participants may find it objectionable.

U-SHAPE TABLE ARRANGEMENT

Many participants and facilitators are accustomed to the presence of a U-shape table arrangement for these sessions, but few know why they are used or why this arrangement is important.

Reasons Why This Arrangement Is Necessary or Important

From the facilitator's viewpoint, it is very important to have a U-shape table arrangement, even when it requires a larger meeting room, since only this arrangement will allow the facilitator sufficient access to participants to apply the interventions just discussed. With a conference table, fewer interventions can be applied; more important is that the facilitator cannot move among the group and establish a nonverbal but positive relationship with all participants.

Use of a U-Shape Arrangement

The major reason for a U shape is to allow the facilitator the freedom to approach any participant freely, without drawing attention. It is a simple and natural movement to walk toward participants who are speaking, to move around within the U shape, and to ask questions while doing so. This should not be done all the time, only periodically throughout the discussion. Then, when there are negative behaviors, it will not be noticed when the facilitator again moves within the group. Exhibit 9.4 shows the suggested design for a U-shape arrangement.

Interventions #1, #4, #5, and #6 can be done from the facilitator's stool position. However, all of the in-session interventions (#1 through #7) can be done while moving within the U-shape arrange-

Exhibit 9.4   U-Shape Table Arrangement

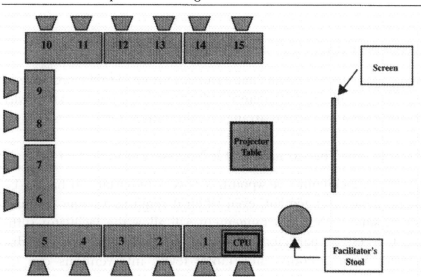

ment. Moving close to the specific participant who is causing difficulty can be done to be close to (or in later stages to invade) the person's personal bubble and thus gain his or her close attention. This will make the interventions far more effective than remaining at the facilitator's stool or at the front of the room.

IDEAL STATE OF FACILITATION

After describing the difficulties that can occur in a facilitation, it should be noted that these are not common. Usually a facilitation session includes a range of behaviors, both positive and negative. There is, however, an "ideal state of facilitation" that sometimes occurs. This is characterized by:

- Conversation being constructive, to the point, and flowing smoothly
- Participants advancing the discussion through their own questions to each other
- Participants setting aside their own personal objections
- Significant progress being made to forming a solution and agreeing upon it, without facilitator assistance
- A rapid flow of comments and an easy development of consensus

This ideal state is something to be desired but rarely to be expected. It comes only when the session has been well managed and group members are comfortable with each other, the objectives they are seeking, and the facilitator's performance.

What should facilitators do when this ideal state appears? They should do nothing, just sit down and observe the progress that the participants are making by themselves. It is during such an ideal state that the meeting's greatest progress will be made. Facilitators should consider this phase to be the result of an excellent performance of their role and should stay out of the way as the participants solve their own problem.

Typically, this ideal state lasts only for a few minutes. At the end, the facilitator can resume guiding the group's discussion. However, it is likely that a quantum leap has been made in the meeting, and often the facilitator will call a break or move on to the next area of discussion.

RESEARCH RESULTS ON EFFECTIVE FACILITATION

In the early 1990s, the University of Georgia's Department of Management researched factors that determined effectiveness of facilitation in electronic environments—that is, using electronic voting systems and related technologies. They surveyed 257 experienced facilitators to determine what skills are most important. The survey is shown in Exhibit 9.5 and is reprinted with permission.

Exhibit 9.5   The 16 Dimensions of Effective Facilitation*

The 16 Dimensions of Effective Facilitation
Robert P. Bostrom and Vikki Clawson, Researchers
The University of Georgia—Department of Management

1. **Promotes ownership and encourages group responsibility**
   The facilitator helps group take responsibility for and ownership of meeting outcomes and results; helps group create follow-up plans in an effort to carry on after the meeting; moves out of the way of group, stays out of their content; turns the floor over to others; permits group to call own breaks; encourages group to evaluate process and technology.

2. **Demonstrates self-awareness and self-expression**
   The facilitator recognizes and deals with own behavior and feelings; is comfortable being self; responds in an emotionally appropriate way, for example, calm under pressure; pays attention to and acts on gut reactions; behaves confidently; behaves honestly—openly admits mistakes and lack of knowledge; shows enthusiasm and personal spirit; keeps personal ego out of the way of the group.

3. **Appropriately selects and prepares technology**
   The facilitator appropriately matches computer-based tools to the task(s) and outcome(s) the group wants to accomplish; selects tools that fit group

---

continues

160

Exhibit 9.5   Continued

makeup; uses technology as tool, not as an end in itself; prepares and tests technology ahead of time; thinks about backup plan in case of technology failure.

4. **Listens to, clarifies, and integrates information**
The facilitator really listens to what the group is saying and makes an effort to make sense of it; clarifies goals, agenda, terms, and definitions with group; backtracks participant's responses; listens for and clarifies the meaning behind responses; remembers previous comments to reconnect information; gathers and integrates information; helps organize information into themes.

5. **Develops and asks the "right" questions**
The facilitator considers how to word and ask the "best" questions; asks questions that encourage thought and participation; develops thoughtful questions on the fly; creates appropriate questions in the technology.

6. **Keeps group focused on outcome/task**
The facilitator has a definite direction and knows where to go next; clearly communicates outcomes to the group; makes outcome visible to the group; keeps group focused on and moving toward its outcome; keeps group's comments relevant to its outcome; demonstrates concern for the group's outcome.

7. **Creates comfort with and promotes understanding of the technology and technology outputs**
The facilitator carefully introduces and explains technology to group; directly addresses negative comments and inconveniences caused by technology; helps group interpret and make sense out of screens and graphs; points out key items on screen; paces review of technology outputs to match group's level of understanding.

8. **Creates and reinforces an open, positive, and participative environment**
The facilitator draws out individuals by asking questions; uses activities and technology to get people involved early on; handles dominant people to ensure equal participation; provides anonymity and confidentiality when needed; acknowledges and is open to group's contributions; creates and reinforces positive energy in the group; uses humor, games, puzzles, riddles, music, and play to enhance open, positive environment.

9. **Actively builds rapport and relationships**
The facilitator demonstrates responsiveness and respect for people; is sensitive to emotions; regularly "reads" the group; watches and responds to nonverbal signals; is empathetic to people with special needs; works to stay in

continues

Exhibit 9.5   Continued

tune with group; helps develop constructive relationships with and among members; puts group at ease; greets and mingles with group; uses group's own words and symbols; moves about in the group.

10. **Presents information to group**
The facilitator gives clear and explicit instructions; uses clear and concise language in presenting ideas; gives group written information, such as handouts, printouts; provides research and background information to the group; presents models and framework clearly; makes sure important information, such as outcomes and standards, is visible to the group.

11. **Demonstrates flexibility**
The facilitator thinks on feet; adapts agenda or meeting activities on the spot as needed; can do more than one thing at a time—handles multiple tasks smoothly; adapts personal style to individual/group; tries new things; is willing to do something different from what originally was planned.

12. **Plans and designs the meeting process**
The facilitator plans the meeting ahead of time; directly includes meeting leader/initiator in planning; develops clear meeting outcomes; designs agenda and activities based on outcome, time frame, and group characteristics; defines and clarifies key roles and ground rules; finds out about group ahead of time; incorporates use of traditional and electronic meeting tools; explores potential changes in agenda ahead of time.

13. **Manages conflict and negative emotions constructively**
The facilitator encourages group to handle conflict constructively; provides techniques to help group deal with conflict; uses technology to gather and check group opinions and agreement level in disputes; helps group gain agreement and consensus on issues; allows group to vent negative emotions constructively.

14. **Understands technology and its capabilities**
The facilitator has an overall conceptual understanding of the technology and knows how to operate the system; clearly understands tools and their functions and capabilities; figures out and solves common technical difficulties; identifies and uses other sources of technical expertise as needed.

15. **Encourages/supports multiple perspectives**
The facilitator encourages looking at issues from different points of view; uses techniques, metaphors, stories, examples to get the group to consider different frames of reference; suggests alternative ways of doing or looking at things; uses the technology to explore diversity and multiple perspectives.

continues

Exhibit 9.5   Continued

16. **Directs and manages the meeting**
    The facilitator leads the group through the meeting process; uses the agenda to guide the group; uses technology effectively to manage the group; sets the stage for meeting and each activity; restricts the meeting process appropriately by setting time limits, enforcing roles and ground rules, limiting choices; provides models, frameworks, and processes to guide group; uses breaks effectively; checks progress and reactions with meeting leader and group.

* **Reprinted with permission.**

10

Electronic Voting Systems*

WHAT ARE ELECTRONIC VOTING SYSTEMS?

In the field of meeting automation systems, there are basically two types of computer-based applications:

1. Anonymous voting systems, which allow participants to indicate their preference, priorities, and perceptions on a given subject
2. Workstation systems, which enable participants to write down ideas on their own workstation; all workstations are networked together, and the totality of all ideas entered (or a subset selected by the facilitator) can be displayed on a projection screen

This chapter deals only with anonymous voting systems, which are the application of choice for Control Self-Assessment workshops.

In addition, we will mention electronic scribing of participants' comments using any popular word processing software.

---

* This chapter first appeared in the May 1997 issue of *CSA Sentinel,* published by The Institute of Internal Auditors. It is reprinted here with permission and minor revisions.

Few special features are required to use electronic scribing—just a good word processor and a computer projection system. It is assumed throughout that the participants' comments are being scribed, possibly in a template-based format (see the section "Template-Based Scribing of CSA Sessions"), and that participants can see (and correct when necessary) the notes that are taken from their comments in a real-time mode.

WHAT ROLE DO ANONYMOUS VOTING SYSTEMS PLAY IN CONTROL SELF-ASSESSMENT WORKSHOPS?

When considered just as voting systems, it would seem that these systems would add marginal, if any, value to a CSA workshop. However, when properly used, anonymous voting can provide critical information that:

- Enables participants to express opinions without fear of retribution
- Shows general patterns of agreement, disagreement, polarity, and confusion
- Enables critical votes to be validated by showing the levels of agreement among voters
- Provides the data needed for the facilitator to conduct consensus discussions, to help participants understand where and why they may disagree, and then to proceed to negotiating between the various interest groups—all without personal involvement or conflict
- Transforms perceptions into usable data, for later documentation to management

For example, let us look at a simple, universal use of voting systems—a Risk Map that measures participants' perceptions of the impact of a risk (assuming it occurs) versus the likelihood that it will occur. Such a map is shown in Exhibit 10.1.

It is clear from the map that two or three risks are critical (i.e., both high impact and high likelihood) to the process in question—

Exhibit 10.1   Basic Risk Map

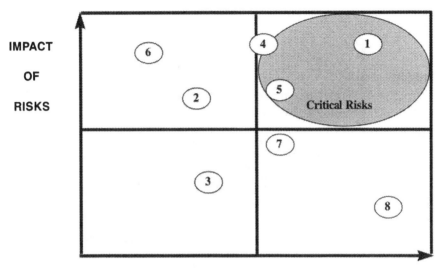

risks #1 and #5, and perhaps #4. The data are taken from the *perceptions* of participants—but what more effective "risk meter" is there?

Note also, in the map, that the top-right quadrant is shaded to indicate that this is the location of the key data we are seeking—the most threatening risks. Many different maps can be constructed, and each must have an interpretation grid constructed to interpret them correctly.

For example, look at Exhibit 10.2 and see how its interpretation is different from Exhibit 10.1. Reading these two maps together, it is clear that although risks #1 and #5 are the most critical, they have a balanced and effective set of controls. Where, then, should internal audit focus its resources? Clearly on risks #4 and #6, which have high threat and an unbalanced/underresourced set of controls.

Note: In Exhibits 10.1 and 10.2, "Threat of Risk" is defined as the voter's "gut-level" perception of a risk's importance; essentially, it is the human perception of impact combined with likelihood of occurrence (e.g., a tornado has higher perceived threat in Tulsa than in Boston). All votes except threat of risk would

Exhibit 10.2   Control Effectiveness Map

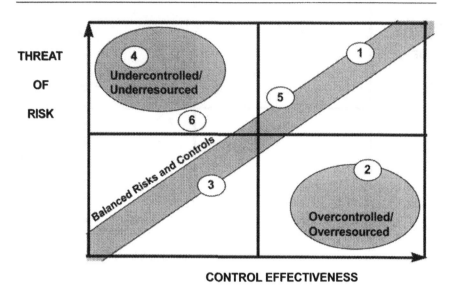

be taken on a scale (e.g., 1 to 9), while threat of risk would be voted using pair-comparison voting for higher accuracy on their priority.

WHAT VALUE DO THESE SYSTEMS DELIVER?

As with any facilitated process, the true value of electronic voting systems is that the results have come from the participants themselves, and therefore are not doubted. Whatever the factual results say—whether it is spoken facts or voting patterns—they have been subjected to group discussion and validation, leading to acceptance of the meeting's results.

As important, these systems provide high impact to participants: Most leave CSA workshops stating that the meeting was one of the best they have ever attended. And most important, these systems allow the workshops to get to real results—action plans to control risks or achieve objectives—in a single day of real-time discussion.

Finally, the inclusion of voting results graphically shows the group's perceptions of the issues very accurately, and at a glance—not just a series of verbal statements in the session notes that, put together, could indicate agreement. The votes are specific, graphic, and undeniable.

WHAT TO LOOK FOR IN AN ELECTRONIC SYSTEM

Many CSA novices assume that all electronic voting systems are essentially the same, but they are not, and it is important to choose the right one for your organization based on three factors:

1. Functionality
2. Ease of use
3. Price

The priorities are in this order for a reason: Unless an organization can afford CSA only by buying the cheapest system, functionality and ease of use are the most critical issues.

Functionality

Some lower-end systems feature only one-dimensional bar graphs, which display the data in piecemeal form. It is up to the reader to put two bar graphs together in their minds, and this is abstract and time-consuming for most people. Therefore, a two-dimensional map is highly desirable; one high-end application even allows four dimensions to be shown, through the use of colors and different-size dots.

Functionality also means the ability to export data to other applications, such as Microsoft Excel, for more complex manipulation. It also means the ability to separate a group's votes into demographic subgroups—field versus headquarters, comparing various age ranges, and so on. The assertion that demographics raise participants' fears that their votes will be less anonymous is generally unfounded. It also means the ability to display *and print* voting outputs easily, and in standard formats that can be exported to popular word processing packages. (See "How to Use Results to Greatest Effect.")

Finally, functionality also can imply various hardware features—such as wired or wireless systems. Wired systems are less expensive but are more difficult to set up, and are less convenient and attractive to participants.

Importance of Simplicity (Ease of Use)

Simplicity is nearly as important as functionality, for it determines whether the system will be used and how broadly throughout your organization. One leading brand is excessively complex to operate due to its basic software architecture; company representatives point to how popular the software is, indicating that it is learnable. But whether a software application *can* be learned is far different from whether it can be learned *easily* and remembered during long periods of nonuse.

The ideal goal of any software—word processing, spreadsheet, graphics or voting—is that it be entirely intuitive in its operation. (Note that Quicken, the home checkwriting system, fulfills this goal. Interestingly, the name of its publisher is Intuit.) One indicator of "intuitive operation" is the operator's manual: Is it constantly required for reference, or can an operator find his or her way through a session without need for look-up?

The basic tests for simplicity or "ease of use" are:

- Can an untrained user sit down at a system, try to operate it, and find some basic success?
- Do trainees retain their learning over the long run, or are repeated trainings required?
- Is the system so simple that operators will be willing to perform this role publicly?
- Will the system's simplicity of use lead to acceptance by system operators, or will there always be hesitancy to undertake this role in an organization?

In summary, therefore, organizations with sufficient capital budget should select the systems that meet their CSA needs, now and in the future. Once the selection has been limited to a few leading contenders, the question to ask is "Is this software both simple (to use) and elegant (in its functionality)?"

INTEGRATION OF CONTROL SELF-ASSESSMENT AND ELECTRONIC SYSTEM SUPPORT

One danger of anonymous voting systems is that they can be easily overused, and the CSA workshop will be less effective. This is a temptation for new users of these systems, and it should be prevented. The reason is that electronic voting is useful in analyzing data that has been gathered, but it does not replace the facilitated discussion in any way. The extreme case would be to compare an ideal CSA facilitated session with a survey collected via anonymous electronic voting: The difference between the two is clearly the process used, and not the voting system. Control Self-Assessment was invented to improve data-gathering of complex issues, and to make it more efficient—automated voting plays no role in gathering this data, only in its analysis.

Therefore, a CSA process should be carefully thought through, and electronic voting should be included only when it adds value to the end results. In one CSA methodology, for example, discussions are held over a period of hours to elicit a large list of business risks, which are then filtered by use of the Risk Map. (See Exhibit 10.1.) Then only the most significant risks are discussed, examining their existing control effectiveness and suggesting new approaches to gain control of the risks. At the end of the session, the Control Effectiveness Map is voted (see Exhibit 10.2) to see where the most work (investment) should be made. This is an appropriate use of voting; voting simply for its own sake is not.

Achieving this integration of CSA process with anonymous voting requires experience, and you may wish to bring in an outside consultant initially, to ensure that you have the most effective and efficient workshop methodology to achieve your goals.

HOW TO USE RESULTS TO GREATEST EFFECT

During the session itself, it is important to display the results of the various votes to participants, so that they can benefit from seeing the input of the full group. Often there will be "outliers" who are surprised to see that their perception is far different from that of other participants.

Having different perceptions is not "bad" and, in fact, can lead to more interesting discussions, even with the outliers remaining anonymous. The facilitator can lead revealing discussions by asking the entire group "Why might someone see this issue so differently? What could lead to that vote?" Meanwhile, outliers may see either that they have not understood the issue or, conversely, that others in the group do not have full information. Either result can be beneficial to the meeting, depending on how well these differences are processed by the CSA facilitator and the participants.

After the session, the voting results should be included in the workshop report. The graphs, maps, and charts will graphically show the opinions of the stakeholders in a process and often are useful in changing a corporate culture from "traditional" (change is discouraged) to "flexible" (instituting change where needed).

TEMPLATE-BASED SCRIBING OF CONTROL
SELF-ASSESSMENT SESSIONS

One of the key benefits of a CSA workshop is the recording of participants' comments. Such records offer verbal testimony of the strengths and weaknesses of given controls, the interdepartmental aspects of business risks, and the details needed to perform accurate and lasting internal audits. In fact, due to the record produced from group discussions of issues, some companies have found a one-day CSA session to replace departmental audits that usually require weeks.

It is difficult, however, to find a "scribe" who can type as fast as people talk. Even if one could be found, the comments would not be categorized in the record itself and would have to be analyzed at a later time. Therefore, the use of CSA templates is a powerful improvement in the scribing process.

A CSA template is a prepared word processing document that has been divided into frames, each frame asking a particular question that is important to the CSA objective. This provides many advantages:

- ○ It allows the facilitator to focus an extensive discussion into discrete sections.
- ○ It allows the scribe automatically to record comments in the right place.
- ○ It helps keep the discussion focused for participants who may tend to wander off the track.
- ○ It greatly assists in creating an organized, insightful report for management.

Exhibit 10.3 shows a sample template based upon a specific CSA process.

But how is a CSA template constructed? Actually, it is quite easy—and very rewarding. Exhibit 10.4 provides the directions. Once the template is built, simply tab to the correct frame section or use the mouse to enter data in the right location.

Exhibit 10.3   Sample CSA Template

Major Objective 1 Engagement Objective: Becoming World-Class Competitior	Major Objective 2 Improving Customer Service
1 Discuss Supporting Objective: *Knowing what our customers most desire in service options and products.*	2.A Performance Data: Actual Effectiveness in Achieving Business Objective Today: _____ (voting score) 2.B Importance to Achieving Major Objective: _____ (voting score)

continues

Exhibit 10.3 Continued.

3. Identify Successes	4. Identify Obstacles
This is the entry into true facilitated data gathering. Participants are asked to name all the successes, big or little, that have occurred in connection with the above supporting objective. The facilitator's role is to get the ball rolling and to keep it rolling. Sometimes this means asking lots of questions, sometimes very few—all depending on the nature of the group.	Once the successes have begun to slow down, the obstacles (or some mixed successes/obstacles) will begin to be volunteered. This is where the facilitator's work really begins: listening to the areas of difficulty or failure, keeping the emotional reactions from starting, preventing blame from entering the conversation, and still reaching for more and more data on what went wrong. After many obstacles have been mentioned, start drawing possible connections between them—that is, start probing for causation (not blame).
5. Major Discussion Points	**6. Management Recommendations**
This area is reserved for discussion of the various points above, in a higher level of analysis. This discussion is meant to raise the perspectives of participants, to see the "raw details" in a more constructive view. This is not meant to push for recommendations, however; the sole purpose is to see the patterns and implications in the successes and obstacles that have been mentioned.	This section is the final phase of discussion for this particular supporting objective. Its purpose is to take the raw data provided, examine the higher points made, and then come up with specific, implementable recommendations for management to consider. Recommendations should have the consensus of the group before being proposed to management.

Exhibit 10.4   Creating a CSA Template

1. **Using Microsoft Word for Windows, create a table of the same dimensions as your sequence of CSA questions.**
2. **Insert exterior and interior borders. (See Toolbar.)**
3. **Click Cursor in table, then Insert - Form Field Text. (You can choose automatic Uppercase, Title Case, and so on under Options - Text Format)**
4. **Insert title for each discussion cell**
5. **Set Tools - Options - Save - Automatic Save Every . . . to 5 minutes; *also* save manually from time to time. (AutoSave only keeps in memory.)**

SUMMARY

Electronic voting systems are a key component to a successful, high-impact CSA session. Many of the same results can be achieved through manual techniques, but only after the session or through long delays during the session. The presence of real-time voting display and analysis is impressive to both participants and management and should be included in CSA programs at the earliest possible stage.

APPENDIX A

A Step-by-Step Guide to Facilitation Meetings: Preparation, Conduct, Reporting, and Follow-Up

Facilitation Guide

I. Preparation	II. Conduct	III. Reporting and Follow-Up
1. Understand and Identify Issues	1. Facilitator is Fully Skilled in the Process	1. Write Participants' Report
2. Establish Clear Objectives for Session	2. Use Correct Facilitation Technology	2. Write Client's Report
3. Determine Methodology for Session	3. Understand Depth and Specificity Required	3. Ensure Action Items Are Completed
4. Prepare for Session	4. Develop Group Consensus and Commitment	4. Establish Plans for Longer-Term Items
5. Schedule Time, Invite Participants	5. Create Record of Words and Voting Data	5. Review Engagement; Seek Additional Needs

CONTENTS

INTRODUCTION

There are many items and issues to be aware of, and to prepare for, when delivering facilitated sessions for clients. This appendix provides a step-by-step guide for each step in the facilitation process; whether the methodology is Control Self-Assessment or strategic planning, the issues presented should be equally applicable.

ORGANIZATION

This appendix is organized in a two-dimensional matrix of information. The three main subject-matter topics—preparation, conduct, and reporting and follow-up, are each divided into five steps, as follows.

Subject-Matter Topics

I. PREPARATION

1. Understand and Identify Issues
2. Establish Clear Objectives for Session
3. Determine Specific Methodology for Session
4. Prepare for Session
5. Schedule Time, Invite Participants

II. CONDUCT

1. Facilitator Is Fully Skilled in the Process
2. Use Correct Facilitation Technology
3. Understand Depth and Specificity Required
4. Develop Group Consensus and Commitment
5. Create Record of Words and Voting Data

III. REPORTING AND FOLLOW-UP

1. Write Participants' Report
2. Write Client's Report

3. Ensure Action Items Are Completed

4. Establish Plans for Longer-Term Items

5. Review Engagement; Seek Additional Needs

For each of these 15 topics, information is provided in an identical format:

A. Topic Description

B. Goals and Objectives to Set

C. How to Achieve These Goals and Objectives

D. Questions and Issues to Remember

This organization is designed for easy reference, and each topic area has complete information on the issues raised. Therefore, there may be some repetition if read from start to finish, as similar issues and solutions are presented under different topics.

Finally, facilitators about to run a session may wish to skim quickly through the "Questions and Issues to Remember" sections within various topics, using it as a preparation checklist.

I. PREPARATION

I.1 Understand and Identify Issues

A. Topic Description

The first step of any consulting engagement is to understand the issues, the industry, the client situation, the objectives to be achieved, and other critical matters that will determine the outcome and the quality of the engagement. When using the CSA approach, however, there is an additional level of complexity: organizing the session in a way that it can be accomplished effectively in a group setting. Business consultants will find that they need to understand the engagement far better at the outset when using CSA than when using traditional "interview—summarize—present" methodologies.

Therefore, the facilitator or facilitative consulting team will have to interview the client to be fully prepared to organize and deliver a well-organized CSA session that asks the key questions first and leaves minor questions for later. This is not as simple as it seems, as the following example will illustrate.

B. Goals and Objectives to Set

The key to CSA is asking key questions to the participants, questions that cut to the core of the subject matter. Be assured that whatever questions are asked will be answered in full detail. Therefore, asking the wrong questions will waste your time and the clients'. To understand what are the right questions to ask, therefore, the facilitator will have to understand:

1. The subject matter of the engagement
2. The "environmental background" of the situation:
    o External factors: market dynamics and so on
    o Internal issues
    o Competitive issues
3. The client's key goals and objectives for the engagement

Then, having the above list in hand, the engagement team will need to organize the information in order to fit the CSA methodology—

that is, a question-and-answer format that provides the right data, at the right level of detail, in the amount of time allocated. (Note that these three factors will compete with each other and compromises will have to be made. For example, insufficient meeting time will mean adjusting the detail level of data; it should never mean compromising whether the right data are obtained.)

C. How to Achieve These Goals and Objectives

With this information, the facilitator needs to form a picture of the engagement that simplifies the issues, to enable a question-and-answer approach. This means prioritizing the problems and the client needs first. Next, it will help if the various issues can be put into a Rubik's Cube arrangement: a multidimensional array of the various dimensions of the engagement.

EXAMPLE: In a manufacturing/distribution engagement, the client is seeking to define an enterprise resource planning solution. Various dimensions can be used to break down and simplify the engagement, as follows:

DIMENSION A: Functional Problems Dimension
o Customer Needs
o Vendor Needs
o Distribution Centers
o Purchasing Function
o Branch Operations
o Logistics

DIMENSION B: Software Implementation Dimension
o Application is insufficient
o Poor installation planning
o Poor logistics focus
o Distribution issues ignored
o Branch issues ignored
o Training not addressed

DIMENSION C: Client Solutions Dimension
- Technology return on investment
- Improving competitive performance
- Increasing inventory turns
- Improving customer service
- Establishing industry leadership

In this situation, any of the dimensions could be attacked first, second, or third. The question is "Which best accomplishes the goals and objectives of the consulting engagement?" In this particular case, the facilitator recommended the following approach:

Six Separate CSA Sessions on the Following Subjects
- Customer Needs
- Vendor Needs
- Distribution Centers
- Purchasing Function
- Branch Operations
- Logistics

In Each Session, Questions to Be Asked on the Following Subjects
- Technology return on investment
- Improving competitive performance
- Increasing inventory turns
- Improving customer service
- Establishing industry leadership

In Each Session, After Each Question Has Been Discussed, Electronic Voting to Ask the Following Questions
- Whether application is insufficient
- Is there poor installation planning
- Is there poor logistics focus

- ○ Are distribution issues ignored
- ○ Are branch issues ignored
- ○ Whether training is addressed

Notice that there were other possible ways to arrange the session. In this case, however, the suggested arrangement best accomplished the client's stated needs and still efficiently inquired into the causes of the problem.

D. Questions and Issues to Remember

The first entry into a complex engagement problem is the hardest. There are numerous issues to understand, environmental information to gather, client needs to prioritize, and so on. There is always a period when the task is simply to gather as much information as possible. Later, once the flood of data has slowed, will come the period of understanding and prioritizing the data. Finally, the consulting team will be able to attack the dimensionality issue— which, in the long run, will be the single most useful tool in simplifying the CSA session, both for facilitators and for participants.

Do not try to rush this process or fix dimensions before all the data are in. You may find later on that the engagement plan will have to be significantly revised, as a result. Do each preparatory step thoroughly, and the issues/questions/dimensions will reveal themselves to the engagement team.

Before proceeding to the next step, ensure that the following questions are settled:

1. Is the CSA approach appropriate for this engagement?
2. Will the client environment support a CSA session? Are there conflicting cultural issues (especially a "command and control" or "divide and conquer" atmosphere) that may lessen the effectiveness of a group facilitation session?
3. Can the information you are seeking be obtained through the CSA question-and-answer approach? For example, a process optimization engagement that is mainly based on

instrumentation data, such as in a manufacturing process, may mean that the answers lie in numbers, not in participants' views.

4. Is your analysis of the issues, problems, and questions acceptable to the client?

I.2 Establish Clear Objectives for Session

A. Topic Description

Once the issues have been understood, identified, and categorized (see last section), it is necessary to establish clear objectives for the upcoming session or series of sessions. This will require meeting with the key client or clients and explaining your engagement approach.

The objective-setting meeting should establish clarity on the purpose, the process, and the expectations for the upcoming sessions.

The Purpose: Are the CSA sessions simply to be used for information gathering? Or will they be used to make recommendations for the best solutions? Or will the participants be asked to make the actual decisions on the approaches to be implemented? It is critical that the client is in agreement with the proposed engagement plan, since a series of CSA sessions will take up a significant amount of management time—and, without proper agreement at the start, could result in outcomes that are not acceptable to management.

B. Goals and Objectives to Set

A formal meeting should be held with the client and key management before the CSA sessions begin, to obtain their approval of the suggested engagement approach.

CSA sessions are high-impact meetings: If the expectations and objectives have been incorrectly defined, then the session probably will succeed in getting the wrong information—that is, it will fail. It is therefore necessary to be crystal clear in defining the goals, objectives, questions, and underlying assumptions of the sessions. If at any time there seems to be a mismatch in any of these areas, the facilitation team should inquire specifically of the client(s) as to whether there is agreement on all issues.

After this meeting, a written report on the meeting and on all agreed items should be distributed to the client and all necessary participants. If the client or team members should disagree with this report upon later review, it is critical to readdress all necessary issues and make sure that both the client and the engagement team are in agreement.

C. How to Achieve These Goals and Objectives

The facilitation team should be present at the objective-setting meeting and should clearly set forth the CSA plan: how and why it is organized in the proposed plan, how it will be conducted, how information will be captured, what reports will be generated and to whom, and what decisions/recommendations are being requested of the participants.

Note that the facilitator and cofacilitator must be present at this meeting and should be the presenters of the above information. The facilitator will be seen as the project leader, and the quality and clarity of this presentation is the basis on which the engagement team will be judged. The cofacilitator, who will support the session through scribing the participants' comments and through supporting the logistics needs of the sessions, should also be introduced to the client and to management.

If a content expert is needed, this is the time to select and/or present that expert to the client management team. This expert will need to meet the standards and expectations of an expert in the industry. On the other hand, the content expert and the client will need to understand that this role is one of support and providing supplementary information, as needed—the content expert is not the facilitator and will play a role in the CSA meetings that is secondary to the facilitator.

Agreement also will be needed as to the level of detail and breadth of coverage in the CSA meeting(s). If there is not sufficient time for in-depth discussion, the client should not be expecting to receive such information in the final report.

The proposed CSA session design should be described in detail, including the priority of the question dimensions. This will be critical for the success of the engagement, since the client's objectives and expectations are very much tied in to the priority of these question dimensions. Note, however, that it is difficult to conduct conversations about multidimensional questions, and the issues will have to be explained carefully to the client.

Participants for each session will need to be identified at this time, at least by category if not by name. Top client management needs to agree to sponsor the sessions and to issue invitations to participants. *Note:* The hardest logistics issue in arranging a CSA session is to obtain the commitment of invited participants to attend. This is solved only by an invitation from a high corporate executive (the CEO or CFO, typically) and by setting a date sufficiently in the future that excuses of unresolvable time conflicts are unreasonable.

D. Questions and Issues to Remember

During the objective-setting meeting, do the client and management seem to understand the CSA engagement plan? Are they just nodding in agreement, or are they involved in the conversation? If there seems to be a lack of communication, it will be necessary to lead the group to a true understanding of the issues, perhaps by using this meeting as an example of the facilitative approach.

Are there conflicting values and goals in the management team? Do these seem to threaten the success of the upcoming CSA session(s)? Is a key manager the center of these problems? Can he or she be met with offline, to understand the particular issues? If not, should that person participate in the meetings with a negative attitude, which could interfere with the success of the meeting?

Can the client, management team, and facilitation team agree on a written document setting forth clearly the purpose, process, and expectations of the upcoming CSA session(s)? Will it be helpful to distribute this document with the invitation to participants?

I.3 Determine Specific Methodology for Session

A. Topic Description

There are different facilitative processes to be used, even within a CSA session; there is also the question as to whether the engagement in question is well suited to a facilitative approach. This section defines these issues more closely, to ensure that a facilitative approach is appropriate in general and that the right facilitative structure is created.

B. Goals and Objectives to Set

The first goal is to determine whether facilitation is the right engagement approach in general. It is easier to answer this question in the negative, that is: "Where is facilitation not appropriate?" than the other way around.

The types of meetings where facilitation is *not* appropriate includes:

o Meetings to implement existing management directives, to be used without question or input from participants. (Participant input will not be used.)

o Meetings to present information, not seeking to use that information to define strategies or tactics to be implemented. (There is not useful participant input.)

o Meetings to choose which participants or departments will have to lose resources (i.e., budget cuts) and which will not. (Here there is no shared objective.)

o Generally, any meetings that are based on a "win-lose" approach and not a "win-win" approach. Also, meetings where orders are simply being handed out to participants for implementation.

Once it is agreed that facilitation is a possible approach (i.e., that none of the above negative qualifiers apply), the next question is to determine which type of facilitation—or which combinations of facilitation methodologies—is appropriate. For this analysis, remember the two key facilitation techniques:

1. ***Strategic Planning:*** Future-oriented, based in creativity techniques. Focused on developing new perspectives and ideas, from which new strategies can be defined and prioritized. Typically, strategic meetings are held at the beginning of a project to set strategic direction or at the end of an engagement to determine solutions to complex problems.

2. ***Control Self-Assessment:*** Present-tense meetings, where business processes are examined in specific detail and pre-planned questions are asked to analyze their current condition. (Where is this process not working? How well is it performing?) CSA meetings can be held as a series of fact-gathering sessions, since their data can be combined into a multidimensional picture of the business process and/or problem.

C. How to Achieve These Goals and Objectives

After conducting the review of engagement issues, dimensions, and so on in Section I.1, "Understand and Identify Issues to Be Examined," a picture should be forming as to the type of information that the engagement is seeking. There are likely to be three types of information:

1. Objective data, such as from financial reports
2. Subjective data, to be gathered from involved individuals
3. Creative ideas/strategies, to be formed by meeting participants after presentation and discussion of the objective and subjective data

Typically, all three types of information are required for consulting engagements. The question here is which are the most important types of information: If it is objective data, then facilitation is not the likely technique to use. If it is creative ideas and strategies, then strategic facilitation is the leading contender to consider as the prime methodology. But if extensive subjective data are needed, CSA is the most likely format to follow. Many situations also require hybrid facilitation approaches, where more than one technique is used or where a combined approach is created.

For example, consider the situation where a major, enterprisewide software implementation has been ongoing for 18 months, when it was promised to be complete in six months. It still is only partly implemented, and those parts are not performing properly—that is, they are not satisfying management's goals. What facilitation approach should be used?

In this situation, consider the need to deliver all the following in an engagement:

- Management's objectives and priorities
- Where and how the software implementation is failing
- What type of fixes are needed for installed components
- What are the needs of the various consituents (customers, vendors, branches, distribution centers, management, etc.)

Here the suggestion would be as follows:

I. Strategic facilitation to determine management's objectives and priorities
II. Series of CSA facilitations to determine
    - What are the needs of the various consituents (customers, vendors, branches, distribution centers, management, etc.)
    - What type of fixes are needed for installed components

This is not the only way to organize such an engagement, and therefore it should be presented to management to determine its acceptability.

D. Questions and Issues to Remember

First, make sure that facilitation is right for this engagement. If facilitation fits the engagement needs technically, determine

191

whether management is willing to have open discussions with candid input from all participants. Ensure that the meetings will not be dominated by senior management (perhaps have different meetings for different staff levels) and whether the meeting will be allowed to proceed according to the participants' information input.

Next, try to use the information previously gathered to formulate a facilitation plan that fits the engagement's stated objectives. Review this plan with client management, ensuring that the engagement team and the client have the same objectives and assumptions.

Make sure that the engagement plan addresses all problem areas, allows participants to formulate a complete solution, and generates a report that will be sufficient to address the problem adequately.

Once the above issues have been settled, develop a specific meeting agenda for all strategic and/or CSA sessions. Review this agenda with the client and with all management involved in each meeting prior to conducting the meeting(s).

Ensure that the strategic facilitation session, if one is to be held, involves a facilitator who is experienced in that methodology. Particularly for a strategic session, ensure that all involved management will be present at the meeting—that is, that all areas necessary for a successful solution are part of the planning meeting. If some managers are absent, they may become barriers to the implementation of the solutions developed at the meeting.

I1.4 Prepare for Session

A. *Topic Description*

No facilitation session can be successful without sufficient advance preparation. This includes having

- An understanding of the session's objectives
- An appropriate methodology defined and agreed with the client
- All necessary information available to run the session
- All required equipment and supplies
- Facilitator(s) who are both skilled in the techniques and familiar with the required information
- Appropriate facilities
- An appropriate participant group
- Clear management support

B. *Goals and Objectives to Set*

Before proceeding with the engagement facilitation sessions, it is assumed that a methodology has been developed that is customized to the particular needs of the engagement and that it has been approved by management. The client's role is critical in the next step—ensuring the attendance of all necessary participants. If the client is not the CEO or CFO, the role will include obtaining session invitations from that (or similar) executive level.

Participants should be chosen from "process owners" (those who are most affected by the meeting's outcomes), any management necessary to ensure the success of the engagement recommendations, and in some cases "process workers" who have specific information that is necessary to defining strategies and process improvements in sufficient detail. When a process or problem cuts across different departments or divisions, then the participant group should include representatives from those areas as well.

C. How to Achieve These Goals and Objectives

Generally, strategic facilitation sessions should have participants from similar levels of responsibility: It is difficult to conduct strategic sessions, which involve abstracting data into higher-level information, when workers and senior executives are both involved. Each has its own ways of seeing the work process, and sometimes a broad vertical slice (i.e., CEO to shopworker) prevents effective communication.

On the other hand, in some CSA sessions a "vertical slice" of process participants is recommended. Consider, for example, the examination of the accounts payable process in a major corporation: Here the entire department should be included (manager to clerks) so that the information gathered about the process is complete and includes all viewpoints. But note that this type of meeting (CSA) is gathering data, while the prior paragraph was discussing strategic idea development: In the first, all necessary levels of staff should be included, while strategic meetings should have no more than two to three contiguous levels of management meeting together.

D. Questions and Issues to Remember

All sessions require preparation for both the participants and the facilitation team. Participants may have to: read material; complete surveys so the session can start with critical information; participate in interviews with facilitators to explore the various facts and attitudes about the problem or business process. Or participant preparation could come at the very beginning of the facilitation, such as a presentation by the engagement team on what the problems are and what is the process being used to remedy the situation.

Similarly, the facilitation team needs to be prepared on the:

o Process to be used at the session
o Roles of the individual consultants
o Subject matter that will be discussed
o Types of support needed by the facilitator during the session

194

The logistics of a successful facilitation meeting require many skills, usually from a very few people. (The typical facilitation team for a CSA meeting, for example, consists of just two members: the facilitator and cofacilitator.) The role of the facilitator is clear: to guide the participants through the various steps of the facilitation process, using group dynamic skills to ensure that the maximum information is contributed. In meetings where electronic voting is used, the facilitator also must conduct the voting and help participants understand the information gained from it; frequently that also will lead to consensus discussions where the reasons for differing views are explored.

The role of the cofacilitator, however, is less well understood. It includes:

- (CSA) Recording participants' discussion comments in word processing software, typically projected in real time while the comments are being entered.
- (Strategic) Assisting the facilitator in writing comments on flipcharts, hanging the flipchart sheets.
- (Electronic voting) Setting up the voting system and testing it fully before the start of the session. (The facilitator is responsible for entering appropriate topics and questions.)
- Ensuring that the facilitation location is appropriate for the meeting: sufficient size, temperature control (thermostat) available, sufficient light but ability to turn lights down or close curtains for projection on screen.
- Arranging the room appropriately (U-shape table arrangement), ensuring that there will be refreshments available (breakfast, morning break, lunch, afternoon break).
- Generally, enabling the facilitator to remain focused on leading the discussion and understanding the key issues of the meeting.

Other areas of preparation include issues regarding electronic voting, if used for the session:

o Does the engagement team own an appropriate hardware/software system? If not, has one been rented with sufficient time to test it and get a replacement if it is defective?

o Are there a enough keypads?

o Have the questions been prepared, tested for appropriateness, entered into the voting software, and *tested on the same machine that will be used during the session?*

o Is all necessary equipment tested and ready: data projector, extension cords (both electrical and VGA cable extensions), power strips, HASPs (software security devices needed by some applications)?

o Has all equipment been connected to the specific computer being used, and been fully tested in a session rehearsal? If not, *do so!* There are many potential failure modes (not knowing how to project the image, computer requiring an unknown password, etc.), and the only way to avoid them is to rehearse the session completely.

o Has a stool been provided for the facilitator?

o Are there sufficient flipcharts, markers, Post-it Note pads, name cards, and copies of the agenda for all participants?

I.5 Schedule Time, Invite Participants

A. Topic Description

Facilitated meetings, whether CSA or strategic in nature, have one key component that can never be left out: the participants. Frequently, however, facilitators simply assume that there will be participants at the meeting. Careful planning and the involvement of the client/sponsor is critical to the success of the meeting, successful implementation of the meeting's recommendations, and the successful outcome of the engagement

B. Goals and Objectives to Set

There are many issues regarding participants at the meeting, including sufficient:

- Number
- Connection with the subject matter
- Managerial level
- Coverage of the facilitation subject matter (e.g., the full business process)
- Interest in the proceedings
- Commitment to a successful outcome
- Time available in their schedule

C. How to Achieve These Goals and Objectives

For a successful facilitated meeting, all the above issues must be addressed. Some are more easily handled, such as sufficient time available in their schedule: This requires invitations going out at least four weeks prior to the planned session(s).

Many of these issues involve the matter of personal commitment on the part of the managers. For example, regarding "sufficient interest in the proceedings": If there is no commitment to the meetings, then participants will not appear. Regarding whether people do not have "sufficient commitment to a successful outcome": If they appear, they will have little interest in the proceedings (poison to a facilitation session); and if they participate in the meeting, they may not be committed to implementation of the group's recommended strategies.

The facilitation team can do little to improve the personal commitment of a manager to having a successful meeting. This is for the client to do, acting as the sponsor of the facilitated engagement for the organization. If the client is the CEO/CFO/process leader, it is up to him or her to ensure both sufficient attendance and sufficiently interested attendees. If the client is not in the leadership position, it is his or her responsibility to enroll such a leader in the political process to bring interested, committed managers to the meeting. Finally, this should be done with finesse and not coercion: Senior managers who are forced to attend a facilitation session against their will are likely to be destructive forces in the meeting.

There are, however, some participation issues that can be determined by the facilitation team:

o Sufficient number (CSA: 6–12; Strategic: 12–20)
o Sufficient connection with the subject matter
o Sufficient managerial level
o Sufficient coverage of the facilitation subject matter (e.g., the business process)

All these issues should be included in the facilitation team's planning for a successful meeting. Although team members are not in control of these issues, they should closely examine these participant characteristics and request assistance from the client if the participants are insufficient in any way.

Remember, if there is a "hole" in the participation at a meeting, there will be the same "hole" in the implementation efforts. Facilitation meetings depend on participation for their success; this is not an issue to be taken lightly.

D. Questions and Issues to Remember

o Has the client or sponsor agreed explicitly to help gain appropriate attendance?

○ Do you have high executive support, if your client/sponsor is not at a high executive level?

○ Have the session dates been planned in advance, by at least four to six weeks?

○ Have invitations been sent out at least four weeks in advance?

○ Have the invitations been sent by the highest-ranking executive possible (the CEO, CFO, or VP of the appropriate area)?

○ Have the invitees been given a rapid-response RSVP date?

○ Has there been telephone follow-up to the invitees by someone whom they know personally?

○ Have those with scheduling difficulties been given high-level support for shifting these responsibilities? If they cannot change prior commitments, should the meeting be changed, or should a substitute representative of that function be invited?

○ Have all tentative commitments been finalized?

○ Have all acceptances been reconfirmed two weeks before the session and again one week before?

○ Have all advance materials been sent out two weeks before the session?

○ Have any required presession materials (e.g., surveys) been received in time?

○ Are there indications of opposition to the session from anyone? If so, has the engagement team leader discussed this with the client/sponsor? Has there been a visit or conversation to resolve any pertinent issues?

○ Do invitees understand the importance of their attendance? Do they understand also that, if they or a replacement do not attend, decisions will be made and implemented without their involvement?

II. CONDUCT

II.1 Facilitator Is Fully Skilled in the Process

A. Topic Description

Without question, the single most important person in a CSA session is the facilitator. Without the proper skills, qualities, values and understanding used to lead the meeting, it is certain to deliver substandard results. Therefore, it is critical that all the above areas of expertise be available for the meeting, assuring the maximum possible results.

This section presents a brief overview of these issues. They are examined in greater detail in Chapter 9 ("Necessary Skills, Qualities, and Values of a Facilitator"), which the reader may wish to review in preparing for a facilitation session. The topical outline of Chapter 9 is as follows:

Basic Values of Facilitation

Meeting Leadership

Facilitator's Mind-set

Helpful Attitudes in Leading a Group

Broadening the Comfort Zone

Managing the Emotions of the Group

Difficult Behaviors by Participants

Understanding and Managing Conflict in the Meeting

Setting Ground Rules

Use of Humor

Meeting Interventions

U-Shape Table Arrangement

Ideal State of Facilitation

Research Results on Effective Facilitation

B. Goals and Objective to Set

For a successful session, the facilitator should be well trained in the facilitation techniques to be used, experienced through actual session leadership, personally mature, and business-experienced.

It is also important for the facilitator to have the right mind-set in understanding his or her role in the session—what it is and what it is not. For example, a facilitator who was previously a subject-matter consultant, with particular knowledge and expertise, needs to know that the session will best succeed without contributions of ideas and opinions from the session leader.

C. How to Achieve These Goals and Objectives

Skills:
The two types of facilitated meetings require different levels of facilitation skills and experience:

- ○ *CSA Sessions:* This is the entry point for new facilitators. Since the session is well structured to follow specific process steps, and since the questions are generally predetermined, the major skills required are those of group dynamics and leadership.
- ○ *Strategic Sessions:* These sessions require a higher degree of skill, since they follow a psychological flow, bringing the participant group from a low/problem perspective to a high/solution perspective, then ask the participants to generate creative ideas and strategies. Questions are not predetermined, and the facilitator depends much more on the "feeling" of the group and their readiness to proceed to the next step in the facilitation process.

Qualities:
The first and most important facilitative quality is the ability to elicit constructive responses from the group. This requires multiple abilities, including the ability to

- ○ Listen closely
- ○ Extract the core meaning of participants' statements, which can often be long-winded and poorly focused

- ○ Sense the direction the conversation is going
- ○ Relate the comments to the meeting's subject matter, if not clear within the comment itself
- ○ Know when to pull more information from the group and when to move to the next step in the process

Numerous other skills are set forth in Chapter 9.

Values:

The list of values that are necessary for a successful facilitator are as follows:

- ○ Asking, not telling
- ○ Gaining consensus
- ○ Patience brings far better results
- ○ Nearly all information can be valuable
- ○ Seeing patterns of discussion and behavior
- ○ Understanding group dynamics
- ○ Commitment to participants
- ○ Neutrality
- ○ Facilitator involvement
- ○ Patience required at all times
- ○ Facilitator as "servant of the group"

(Each of these subjects is described in detail in Chapter 9.)

Understanding:

This topic is divided into three types of understanding:

1. Subject-matter understanding
2. Process understanding
3. Emotional understanding (group dynamics)

Subject-matter understanding typically comes from experience in the field being discussed, presession study of the business environment and terminology, and general business experience and maturity. With extensive business experience, "maturity" means that the facilitator can see patterns in the discussion that are reaching toward specific issues seen in past sessions, but occurring in different industries. The mature facilitator will be able to see this parallel and draw upon past experience to lead the group to stating their concerns and perhaps seeing ways to avoid or remedy those concerns.

Process understanding means that the facilitator knows the process thoroughly and is able to move through its various steps with certainty and correctness. For example, many groups try to raise solutions to problems at the beginning of sessions when they are asked simply to state the problems that are occurring. The facilitator's role is to inform them that this process step is merely to list the problems and that solutions will be discussed later; also, that any ideas envisioned during this step should be written down for later contribution during the idea-generation step of the process. In this way, the facilitator has kept the process moving along its own track and still has not lost the support (or the ideas) of the participants.

In a session involving many people, there is factual communication and emotional communication. The facilitator must understand both sides of this equation and be able to take appropriate steps when either area shows signs of going off-track. For factual communication, this means bringing the subject matter back into focus. For emotional communication, it means building and constantly rebuilding a positive, constructive meeting dynamic. When certain individuals try to change or disturb the meeting dynamic, it is up to the facilitator to deal with this appropriately and discreetly. (Refer to the Chapter 9 sections on ground rules, humor, and interventions to handle these issues.)

D. Questions and Issues to Remember

To ensure full preparedness for an upcoming session, facilitators should review the contents of this section and, if they feel more detail is needed, Chapter 9 as well. The following topic areas should be questioned internally, to ensure that the facilitator has full understanding and feels fully prepared:

From Chapter 9: "Necessary Skills, Qualities, and Values of a Facilatator"

Basic Values of Facilitation

Meeting Leadership

Facilitator's Mind-set

Helpful Attitudes in Leading a Group

Broadening the Comfort Zone

Managing the Emotions of the Group

Difficult Behaviors by Participants

Understanding and Managing Conflict in the Meeting

Setting Ground Rules

Use of Humor

Meeting Interventions

U-Shape Table Arrangement

Ideal State of Facilitation

Research Results on Effective Facilitation

From this overview of facilitator process skills:

Training

Mind-set

Skills

Qualities

Values

Understanding

- Subject-matter understanding
- Process understanding
- Emotional understanding (group dynamics)

If facilitators feel comfortable in understanding these areas, then they are prepared to conduct the meeting. Although unexpected comments, reactions, and discussions may arise, this subject matter should provide facilitators with the tools, techniques, and skills to handle the unexpected.

II.2 Use Correct Facilitation Technology

A. *Topic Description*

In nonelectronic facilitation meetings, "technology" refers to the use of Post-it Notes for idea gathering, flipcharts, colored dots for voting on strategic priorities, and the like. In an "electronic facilitation" meeting, however, significant process improvements can be achieved through use of electronic voting systems. These will be briefly reviewed here; the reader should also consult Chapter 10 for more specific information.

Please note that other forms of electronic support—teleconferencing, videoconferencing, computer-based idea-sharing systems—are not discussed here. The basic assumption of this book is that a facilitation session is "same time/same place," obviating the need for remote conferencing systems. Also, the author's experience suggests that computerized idea-sharing does not add significant value to facilitation sessions and that manual techniques led by a skilled facilitator can be equally effective.

The value of anonymous, electronic voting systems, however, adds exceptional value to facilitation meetings when used appropriately and not excessively. These issues are examined below and also in Chapter 10.

B. *Goals and Objectives to Set*

For electronic voting systems to add significant value to a meeting, they should satisfy these requirements:

o They should not be physically cumbersome.
o Their use should not dominate the meeting.
o They should be anonymous, protecting the identity of voters.
o They should be flexible.
o They should be easy for the facilitator to use.
o Data displays should be easily understood by participants.
o The maximum possible use of voting data should be available.

C. How to Achieve These Goals and Objectives

They should not be physically cumbersome: Both wired and wireless voting systems are available. Technically, wired systems are more reliable in session use, since votes are rarely lost in transmission, as is possible in wireless systems. From the participant's viewpoint, however, wireless systems are more "modern" and the facilitation room is less disturbed with wires and connectors. As a bottom-line recommendation, the facilitator should choose the wireless systems for the above reasons and for two others:

1. Wireless systems are easier to transport.
2. Wireless systems are easier to set up before the facilitation meeting.

Their use should not dominate the meeting: New facilitators may be tempted to use voting technology excessively. With practice, facilitators soon learn that voting should be used only as a summary analysis of ideas and strategies developed through the group discussion phases of a session. Although voting may take up only 10 to 20 percent of a meeting's time, often participants perceive it to contribute a majority of the value. If, however, voting is used excessively, it will tend to annoy participants and lower their estimation of a session's value—that is, they will see the session as "an automated survey."

They should be anonymous, protecting the identity of voters: The power of voting is in its ability to quantify the individual and group perceptions of the participants anonymously. Without anonymity, participants will feel intruded upon and will not vote candidly on their perceptions of issues. *Note:* If senior management suggests that voting results be provided on each individual, facilitators should always refuse—even to the point of sacrificing the engagement. Not only is there an ethical issue in showing the individual results to management, doing so will erect a barrier between the facilitator and the group even if the management arrangement is kept secret.

They should be flexible: There are a handful of good voting systems, but only one or two of them provide true flexibility during session use. All systems claim flexibility, but only the facilitator can judge the truth. It is strongly recommended that facilitators have trial periods for any system they are considering using during which they should exercise the system extensively. Once they understand the basics of a voting system, the choice will become obvious as to which system they prefer.

They should be easy for the facilitator to use: Ease of use is a much-used, and much-abused, term: Every software provider claims ease of use, and few facilitators find it to be a reality. Only full-scale sessions or mock sessions can reveal whether a facilitator will be able to handle a software system when conducting a session. Again, a trial purchase period is recommended, with facilitators taking time to exercise the system rigorously.

Data displays should be easily understood by participants: The facilitator is only the operator of the system—it is the participants and the client who are the true recipients of a system's value. This falls into two uses: during a session and in the session report delivered later to the client. Our focus is on use during the facilitation session, since most system deficiencies in reporting can be remedied through use of spreadsheet and graphics software. Therefore, our view is simple: Participants should be able to view a voting screen and immediately get valuable insight from the data displayed. If there is a deeper layer of insight, it should be easily demonstrated and explained by the facilitator. If a voting system cannot provide easy-to-understand data views, it should be avoided.

The maximum possible use of voting data should be available: Voting data can be displayed in many different ways, even for the same voting inquiry. There are two basic views:

1. Main Profile Map: A display of all voting topics on a two-dimensional (sometimes three-dimensional) voting display. Each topic is shown in an X,Y position that is the average of all voters' individual opinions.

2. Scatter Map: A supporting display, where a single topic's votes are displayed on the same X,Y grid, but showing all individual votes that formed the average position on the Main Profile Map—with votes *anonymously* displayed. This map is critical in determining whether the group's average X,Y position for a topic results from true consensus, or whether there is confusion/disagreement/organizational differences that are averaged into the averaged display. (*Note:* Sometimes "scatter map" is used to mean "main profile map" by software systems that do not have the type of scatter map described here.)

Beyond the basic views, two other displays are quite useful:

1. Demographic View: If voters come from different organizational or personal backgrounds, frequently they are asked to indicate those backgrounds by multiple-choice voting; then these results are cross-tabulated to categorize the votes shown in the Main Profile Map. Very few systems display these results in a logical and simple way. Our preference is for a subdisplay that shows demographic groups, averaged within each sub-group, displayed simultaneously around the full group's average location.

2. Individual Voting Map: Many software providers believe that individual voting maps should not be provided, for reasons of anonymity. However, we believe these are critical to having a positive effect on the voting consensus within a group—but they must be handled confidentially. Thus, two sets of data can be provided to participants:

    ○ A package of the full group's voting data: main profile map, plus scatter maps and demographic maps for all topics. These can be printed out once, then photocopied and distributed openly to all participants.

    ○ A copy of each individual's main profile map, showing how that specific person voted on all topics. This should be printed and distributed confidentially, so only that individual can see the private and anonymous voting map.

Providing both public and private sets of data has a high impact on participants: They can now compare their own, confidential voting with that of the group as a whole. Frequently, for example, CEOs will see for the first time how greatly their views differ from the rank-and-file—without the ability to blame others or punish them. Often this causes upper management to loosen up on issues and many times can bring about consensus on an issue—not full agreement, but sufficient agreement and acceptance of others' views that the issue can move forward.

D. Questions and Issues to Remember

If using electronic voting technology, review these require-ments carefully and score your system's appropriateness:

- They should not be physically cumbersome.
- Their use should not dominate the meeting.
- They should be anonymous, protecting the identity of voters.
- They should be flexible.
- They should be easy for the facilitator to use.
- Data displays should be easily understood by participants.
- The maximum possible use of voting data should be available.

II.3 Understand Depth and Specificity Required

A. Topic Description

As described in Chapter 5, five dimensions of session design compete with each other in obtaining sufficient and correct data:

1. Time allotted for session(s)
2. Breadth of coverage (scope)
3. Depth of detail
4. Coverage of cross-section of employees
5. Data sufficient to cross-validate results

Therefore, when focusing on depth of detail, it is critical that the facilitator understand the interplay of the other four factors and ensure that it is even possible to obtain the level of detail desired by the client given the time allotted for meetings.

B. Goals and Objectives to Set

Given the two different types of facilitation that can be used, the facilitator also should be aware of their different requirements to deliver the appropriate level of detail:

- For strategic sessions, the depth of detail increases with the time allotted for each session.
- For CSA sessions, depth of detail involves two factors:
  1. Sufficient time for each topic-focused session, with a sufficient total number of sessions to provide the full set of data desired
  2. Establishing the right level of detail in participants' responses, right at the beginning of the session

C. How to Achieve These Goals and Objectives

It is critically important to review the five dimensions, shown above, with the client when planning the session or series of sessions. This is the only point when unreasonable client expectations can surface and be discussed and resolved. Once a facilitation plan has been proposed and accepted, the next opportunity to discuss the sufficiency of detail is when a session—or, even worse, the full series of sessions—has been completed.

Once discussed and agreed, the facilitation team and the client will understand the need to prioritize the five dimensions. This will allow the facilitator to make adjustments that enable sufficient detail to be achieved within the allotted time, without sacrificing other values that are important to the client.

Time management during a session is important in achieving the defined level of detail, and it is therefore important that the entire facilitation team understand the need for a smoothly functioning session. All should be well rehearsed in their roles, even if it is only to assist in hanging charts on the wall. Scribes, particularly important in CSA sessions, must be able to glean the important content in a participant's statement and enter it into the word processing system with a minimum of interaction or involvement from the facilitator. (For example, facilitators often repeat phrases to be entered into the session record when working with new scribes; this, of course, takes up valuable session time.)

The facilitator's role in obtaining the right level of detail, particularly in a CSA session, is to ensure that participants are told whether their comments have too high—or too detailed—a perspective. The easiest way to describe appropriate levels of detail is the analogy of flight altitude—that is, "That's a 500-foot view of the issue. Could we raise it a bit, perhaps to 1,000 feet?"

It is also important that the facilitator keep the "altitude check" in mind throughout the meeting; often there will be "altitude creep," where comments drift to higher or lower levels of detail. Specific comments should be made to the group to correct this.

Another way to adjust the level of participants' input is to ask either of the following questions:

o To raise perspective: "What does that mean? What does that give you?"

212

o To lower perspective: "How is that done? What are the elements of that comment?"

D. Questions and Issues to Remember

Discuss the five dimensions of session planning with the client, with a primary focus on level of detail:

1. Time allotted for session(s)
2. Breadth of coverage (scope)
3. Depth of detail
4. Coverage of cross-section of employees
5. Data sufficient to cross-validate results

Ensure that you have the client's agreement on the level of detail expected or that the client is willing to alter one of the other dimensions to make suitable adjustments. In most cases, the first three dimensions are the primary considerations; covering a cross-section of employees or cross-validating results is only rarely important to clients.

The facilitation team should recognize their need to thoroughly understand the session and to perform their roles with a minimum of wasted time.

The scribe should be well practiced in entering participants' comments, even if this means practicing prior to the session (e.g., scribing a TV newscast).

The facilitator should know the exact level of detail required by the client and the engagement plan, and should be prepared to communicate this requirement to the session as a whole or to individuals who are providing information of too high or too low a perspective.

II.4 Develop Group Consensus and Commitment

A. Topic Description

A facilitation session is not complete without the development of group consensus in the results generated. The basic output of a session is a large volume of information, typically derived from participants' comments. Such comments, however, are not sufficient to define a strategy to remedy the problems under discussion or to implement the strategies developed during the session. It is up to the facilitator to assist the group in understanding their areas of disagreement, to lessen the disagreements where possible, and to formulate acceptable strategies and recommendations even when certain disagreements remain.

B. Goals and Objectives to Set

The first goal is to ensure that the group understands the difference between agreement and consensus. For this purpose, consensus is defined as "sufficient agreement to move forward" with a strategy or a recommendation. The definition is simple, but its implementation is more complex. To develop a true consensus, the following steps are necessary:

o The discussion of a topic should have a complete airing of participants' views, even when there is clear disagreement on the main subject or on key underlying principles.

o Participants should all understand that disagreement is natural and acceptable, even in a group decision-making situation.

o The facilitator should be seeking the sources of disagreement during the discussion, both through a continuing, personal review of comments as they are made and also through open discussion with participants on these underlying causes for disagreement.

o Facilitators should not try to smother disagreement or gloss it over. Without clear statements of each participant's position, it will not be possible to keep all participants emotionally involved in the meeting and its outputs.

○ When anonymous electronic voting is used, the facilitator should display areas of disagreement using the tools provided by the voting software.

○ When true causes of disagreement are discovered—whether through discussion or through voting displays—they should be discussed neutrally with the entire group of participants. The goal is to help all participants understand each other's perspectives, not to change their perspectives.

C. How to Achieve These Goals and Objectives

Consensus-building voting software features include the following displays, which are more fully described in Section II.2 of this appendix:

○ Main Profile Map: Showing the relative positions of all topics using the average of all voting scores.

○ Scatter Map: A supporting display, where a single topic's votes are displayed on the same X,Y grid, but showing all individual votes that formed the average position on the Main Profile Map—with votes *anonymously* displayed.

○ Demographic View: If voters come from different organizational or personal backgrounds, frequently they are asked to indicate those backgrounds by multiple-choice voting; then these results are used to analyze the votes shown in the Main Profile Map.

○ Individual Voting Map: Such maps are critical to having a positive effect on the voting consensus within a group, but they must be handled confidentially.

Either through an in-depth discussion or through use of software tools, the facilitator's objective is to show that:

o There is disagreement in any group discussion.

o The disagreement has logical roots based on participants' various experiences *and is acceptable.*

o It is still possible to recommend a strategy or action plan, even with continuing disagreement.

o Such recommendation requires each participant to appreciate the possibility of varying views and values and to accept that not every disagreement is a "show-stopper."

Once these points have been discussed, the group is free to view their disagreements from a nonemotional perspective. The goal of this consensus discussion is not to cause participants to change their votes; rather, it is to help them understand the varying perspectives in the meeting and be willing to make group decisions even in the presence of such differing views.

The consensus discussion is actually a microversion of the facilitation process as a whole. Within a smaller topic area (e.g., "Disagreement on Recommendation A"), the three-step, core facilitation model is being used:

1. Knowledge
2. Consensus
3. Commitment

(For more information on this core model, see Chapter 2.)

Here the facilitator's skills are directed at eliciting the knowledge of the disagreement and sharing that knowledge among all participants. With the exception of secret or personal agendas, which occur less frequently than expected, this exposure of different views leads to consensus and commitment. It will, however, require both time and patience.

This phase of the discussion also will require the support of the various voting software tools. The facilitator's task is to use the demographics feature to find the "dimension(s) of difference" among the participants—that is, underlying causes that are easily shown to affect their perspectives on the problem. Dimensions of difference could include:

- Department or division
- Level of responsibility
- Industry experience
- Time with the company
- Geography represented (especially field location versus headquarters)
- Age

The applicability of these dimensions can be elicited through discussion and often through voting demographics. The goal in the voting approach is to have a single demographic that shows wide disagreement among its subgroups; when the demographic display has no clear separation between groups, that demograph is not a dimension of difference. When this are shown on-screen, it is clear to participants why they see the situation differently. This opens the door to developing a consensus position or recommendation.

It is important for both facilitators and participants to understand that complete agreement on all issues is not necessary to formulate recommendations. The goal is twofold:

1. To develop consensus on only those issues that are specifically required for the recommendation
2. To agree that the areas of agreement are sufficient to move forward with a recommendation, and outweigh the areas of disagreement

D. Questions and Issues to Remember

To help the session participants come to a consensus view and recommendation, the facilitator should proceed through the following steps:

1. Full discussion of the topic area
2. Exposure of all major areas of disagreement
3. Distillation of the areas of disagreement into categories or causes of the disagreement
4. Further discussion of these causes of disagreement, with the goal of all participants understanding the many perspectives present at the session
5. Continuing the recommendation discussion, but now directed toward forming a basic consensus of what is agreeable to the participant group—even in the presence of different personal views on the subject
6. Developing a final, consensus-based recommendation that is either:
   - Agreeable to each member of the session
   - Acceptable to each member, after understanding the various perspectives on the problem that have been expressed

II.5 Create Record of Words and Voting Data

A. Topic Description

The value of a facilitation session lies not in the experience of the participants for those few hours but in the recommendations and commitment built during the session. This means that there must be an accurate record of the session, both to inform management of the strategies and recommendations and also to provide to participants a written "contract" of what they agreed.

It is therefore necessary to have the tools and skills to create a written record of the session. This record must be developed in real time (during the session itself). It also should be developed in the sight of the participants, so that they can voice their disagreements with statements recorded incorrectly. By the end of the facilitation session, the record that has been built in full view of the group will become the basis of session reports and will clearly have the support of those participating in the session.

B. Goals and Objectives to Set

Certain key requirements go into creating a written session record:

- The record should be visible to all participants while being created.
- It should be complete and accurate.
- It should be sufficiently detailed that later readers will understand the evolution of the discussion, and the progress made from disagreement to consensus.
- The writing process should not hinder or impede the progress of the session.
- It should include either participants' actual comments (perhaps simplified, with speakers' assent) or the flipchart notes made by the facilitator as a result of their comments.
- If voting technology is used, the data displays that are shown to participants also should be recorded for inclusion into the session report.

C. How to Achieve These Goals and Objectives

There are two basic approaches to session recording:

1. Flipchart notation by the facilitator
2. Word processor data entry by the cofacilitator

These two approaches will be examined separately.

Flipchart Notation by the Facilitator

This approach is used in all strategic sessions and occasionally in CSA sessions. The reason for its use in strategic planning is that the flipchart pages, which make up the sequential record of the meeting, are mounted on the meeting room walls; they remain there throughout the session and are used for later reference and inspiration when the group is asked to generate creative ideas and strategies to solve problems or develop new approaches.

The notes made on these flipcharts by the facilitator must be accurate and summarize the participants' comments. When they are not accurate, the group will frequently give signals of disapproval. The facilitator should be sensitive to these signals and ask what the correct phrasing might be.

Facilitators also should use different marker colors, changing color when recording different speakers' comments. This enables participants to distinguish one speaker's comments from another and to develop a more individualized understanding of the issues.

Once a flipchart page is complete, the cofacilitator or a volunteer from the participant group should mount it on the wall next to the prior sheet. All sheets should be numbered sequentially so that the meeting's discussion sequence can be represented correctly in the final report.

Word Processor Data Entry by the Cofacilitator

Since CSA sessions do not have a creative idea-generation phase, comments do not have to be recorded and displayed on the meeting room walls. Therefore, it is far simpler and more accurate to maintain an online, real-time record of the session by use of a word processing software application.

Typically, a CSA session will be highly structured. The main topic area, subtopics, and specific questions to be asked will be prepared in advance. For the most accurate written record, therefore, the cofacilitator should enter the topic areas and questions, ready for easy recording of participants' responses during the session. An example of such a prepared approach might be the following:

SAMPLE PRESESSION CSA FILL-IN SCRIPT
TOPIC A: NECESSARY IMPROVEMENTS TO PHYSICAL PLANT

Subtopic 1: Manufacturing Area
Question 1: What Is the Current Physical Plant Like?
Question 2: What Is Appropriate in the Current Layout?
Question 3: What Is Wrong with the Current Layout?
Question 4: What Changes or Fixes Are Recommended?

Subtopic 2: Purchasing, Inventory, and Receiving Areas
Question 1: What Is the Current Physical Plant Like?
Question 2: What Is Appropriate in the Current Layout?
Question 3: What Is Wrong with the Current Layout?
Question 4: What Changes or Fixes Are Recommended?

Subtopic 3: Sales, Marketing, and Finance Areas
Question 1: What Is the Current Physical Plant Like?
Question 2: What Is Appropriate in the Current Layout?
Question 3: What Is Wrong with the Current Layout?
Question 4: What Changes or Fixes Are Recommended?

Subtopic 4: Executive Areas
Question 1: What Is the Current Physical Plant Like?

Question 2: What Is Appropriate in the Current Layout?

Question 3: What Is Wrong with the Current Layout?

Question 4: What Changes or Fixes Are Recommended?

Once this script is ready, it should be installed on the session computer, typically a laptop that also has the voting software installed. During the session, the cofacilitator will act as scribe, entering comments within each appropriate section. The facilitator's role is to ensure that the comments entered are accurate and complete and to correct them when necessary; with beginning scribes, the facilitator may need to dictate each comment word for word.

At the end of the session, the "raw data" entered by the scribe can be handed out to participants, if necessary. Usually that is not required, and participants receive a more complete and error-corrected version a week or two later, including all voting data. This version is also distributed to management—with participant names listed as part of the meeting but never attached to individual comments or votes.

If there is a series of CSA sessions, the engagement team will need to develop a higher-level report to management. This will summarize and distill the results gained from the individual CSA sessions, bringing a higher-level set of recommendations to management. It also will highlight the differences between different groups' recommendations and perhaps link those to their different geographical locations, functional responsibilities, and management/staff levels.

D. Questions and Issues to Remember

○ Has a method been selected for recording comments from participants?

○ Are the tools necessary for that recording arranged for?

○ Do the facilitator and cofacilitator understand their roles and have the necessary skills and experience to perform them?

○ Is the form of the final report already understood, and does the session recording approach appear likely to satisfy the needs of that final report?

○ Do participants understand that there will be a record made of the meeting but that all comments made will be recorded anonymously?

○ Has the voting software been set up to conduct the right type of voting and to be able to report the voting in a graphical display? (This should include the main profile map, the scatter map, and the demographic view but not the individual profile map.)

III. REPORTING AND FOLLOW-UP

III.1 Write Participants' Report

A. Topic Description

Once the facilitation session is complete, all participants must have a record of the session for future reference. There are many reasons for this written session report. It serves as a:

o Record of what was said
o Reference point in case of future uncertainties or disagreements
o Document to memorialize the agreements made during the meeting

Participants' reports are relatively simple to generate and are well worth the effort in terms of future implementation of agreements made.

B. Goals and Objectives to Set

The first issue is whether the report should be simple or complex. Participants' reports should be simple and clear, with a minimum of after-the-fact analysis. Essentially, such a report is simply a written record of the comments recorded on flipcharts or in the scribed record, plus the voting data. More complex reporting will be required in the final client's report, which is described in Section III.2.

The participants' report should be:

1. Distributed quickly: Within one to two weeks.
2. Accurate: An exact record of comments made during the meeting. This accuracy is enhanced by the participants' opportunity during the session to correct flipchart or scribed comments, which are visible to them during the recording process.
3. Complete: The entire record should be included in the participants' report. Even apparently off-subject discussions are

important, since they were part of the thought process in the meeting. Although these comments may not seem important to management or readers not attending the meeting, they will be important to the participants who made them. (The only exception is for comments that were made by the group with the expectation of confidentiality, such as candid discussions of management issues that could reflect negatively on the members of the meeting. In this case, the facilitator should make a commitment of confidentiality and should keep it.)

C. How to Achieve These Goals and Objectives

The basic principle of participants' reports is that they act as a reinforcement of the meeting experience. Therefore, they should not go beyond the actual content of the meeting itself—editorial comments and analytical insight will only serve to weaken this report's purpose.

The sole addition to the meeting data is the need for written interpretations of the voting maps that were created during the meeting. Here the interpretation is necessary to establish a record of the meaning of what was voted, which will be more useful to the participants than simply having a graphical display or spreadsheet record of the votes. This interpretation should be simple and clear and should duplicate the interpretation comments made by the facilitator at the time the votes were first displayed in the meeting. If the facilitator sees other issues later, they should be clearly labeled as such in the report as new material. Without that clarity, participants will notice unfamiliar data, and it will weaken their commitment to the veracity of the written report.

The participants' report, being a relatively simple record of the meeting, can be written in a short time. This is especially true of CSA reports, since the session usually is recorded simultaneously by a scribe using a word processing application. This means that the participants' report will mainly require editing, spell-checking, and formatting; also, the voting information must be inserted into the word processing document.

Not only can the report be written quickly, it should be. The sooner participants receive this report, the sooner the meeting has closure. Participants should have a brief period after receipt of the report in which they can call out any inaccuracies; once that period has passed, however, the report is now a formal record of the meeting. This will be helpful to many parties:

- To the client, in understanding the progress of the engagement
- To the participants of that session, who will now have a document that retains the data and insights that were exchanged
- To the facilitation team, who can study the report to see if their facilitation approach is fully effective—and, if not, to take corrective steps in future meetings.

Recording a strategic session is simple: Flipcharts and markers are the only tools needed, plus masking tape to mount them on walls. In CSA sessions, however, the needs are more complex:

- Laptop computer
- Data projector
- Word processing application that can display in "full-screen" mode (e.g., Microsoft Word)
- Most important, a scribe who can understand and distill participants' comments to their core meaning and who can type reasonably accurately and quickly

D. Questions and Issues to Remember

- What type of recording will be used during the session— flipcharts or electronic?
- If electronic scribing is used, who will be the scribe? Does that person have the ability to compose comment entries by him- or herself, or will the facilitator have to distill the comments? Can the person type well?

○ If electronic scribing is used, will it be displayed to the group as it is written? This is strongly recommended, since it offers the participants a chance to edit on the spot, which is preferable to later editing. It also decreases the possibility of later loss of team commitment, if comments are changed significantly during the editing process.

○ Note that tape recording of sessions is *not* recommended—participants will see this as a threat to their anonymity, since tapes could be given to management.

○ Are the facilitator and cofacilitator clear on each other's roles during the meeting, and are they comfortable with the teamwork necessary for accurate scribing?

○ Does management understand the scope of participants' report? Are other types of information expected in those reports? If so, has this been discussed and settled in discussions with the client? (Note that higher-level reporting will be provided to management; that topic is discussed in the Section III.2.)

III.2 Write Client's Report

A. *Topic Description*

A facilitation session, whether strategic or CSA, is a momentary experience. For certain objectives, it has incomparable value: understanding of the entire range of perspectives of an issue, building strategies and action plans, and generating team consensus and commitment. These benefits, however, reside only within the participant group.

For the benefit of the sponsoring organization as well as for the ongoing implementation of the recommendations resulting from the meeting, a higher-level report must be written. This report should feature the insights, strategies, and plans gathered in the single session or in the series of sessions that were conducted for the client. The main value of the client's report, however, is the analysis and insight of the consulting team, beyond the simple discussion-reporting level of the participants' report. This analysis will link the facilitation results with the engagement's scope and objectives. In addition, recommendations should be made to the client that are based on the participant recommendations but that affect the client organization more broadly.

B. *Goals and Objectives to Set*

The first objective is that the client's report should be an in-depth, high-value document. To satisfy this requirement, the report should include:

- A distillation of the facilitation session(s) and their recommendations
- Observations on the cultural issues observed in the facilitation sessions
- Comments, where appropriate, on the general tone of the facilitation(s)
- Summaries of the recommendations from various sessions
- Listings of all ongoing commitments made during the facilitation session(s)

- A multidimensional analysis, where appropriate, of how recommendations and discussions varied across different sessions (e.g., geographical, functional, responsibility differences, etc.)
- High-level recommendations that include the consulting team's input, based on all research performed (facilitation sessions, interviews, data analysis, etc.)

C. How to Achieve These Goals and Objectives

The creation of the client's report will require the input of all consultants involved in the project. Facilitation may have been used for the entire scope of the project or only for a part of a greater scope, accompanying traditional consulting techniques. Whichever the case, this is the stage at which all research, analysis, comments, voting maps, and other information needs to be gathered together.

The collective information from the consulting engagement should be reviewed by the engagement's senior consultants, to notice trends and factors that may not have been stated specifically during the research (facilitative and nonfacilitative). These observations are highly valuable and should lead to recommendations for higher-level organizational attention.

When reviewing facilitation data, two approaches may prove helpful:

1. The "big table" approach: This technique involves bringing all facilitation session reports, interview results, and research/analysis into a single room with a large table. By spreading all results out simultaneously, the consulting team often can draw parallels and inferences that are more difficult to see in a linear-analysis mode.

2. The consultants' facilitation session: In another nonlinear approach, often it is helpful to have all engagement consultants participate in an informal facilitation session to analyze the results they have obtained. In this case, the facilitation should be guided by the engagement proposal and project outline. By assembling all consultants into a single

room after they have reviewed the entire set of materials, each consultant will be able to draw inferences and conclusions across areas of consulting expertise.

The "consultants' facilitation" is likely to reveal areas highlighted by the initial research as well as areas that should have been highlighted. Often these informational voids will reveal areas of *omission* that are critically valuable to the client, while traditional consulting techniques frequently obtain data on problems of *commission*.

It is also important that the consulting team reread participants' comments during the facilitation sessions, not just the recommendations and voting data. Often their comments have significant value, value that is understood more easily at the conclusion of the research phase than during the session itself.

D. Questions and Issues to Remember

With these techniques, the consulting team should be able to write a client's report that includes:

- A review of the problem under study and the project scope
- A description of the research methods used
- An overview of the facilitation session(s) and results obtained (not the complete results)
- A section that explains the voting methodology used, the voting results and interpretations of all voting data, and patterns of voting that can be shown across multiple facilitation sessions
- A summary of other research data
- Higher-level recommendations from the participants, and also from the consulting team
- Implementation suggestions reflecting both the initial project scope and related issues that were discovered during the research phase
- Proposal for implementation of the suggested solutions

III.3 Ensure Action Items Are Completed

A. Topic Description

The engagement does not end with the client's report, as a practical matter. Once meetings have been held, there is the remaining issue of implementing action items agreed during the meetings. The issue may appear to be a client matter, but failure to implement will always affect the client organization's view of the consulting team's effectiveness.

In this section we discuss implementation of action items and short-term commitments. This is distinguished from longer-term strategies, which are discussed in Section III.4. On the whole, major strategy recommendations are monitored more effectively than short-term commitments; it is common, for example, to hold regular progress meetings for longer-term commitments. It is the short-term action items, therefore, that often fall between the cracks—but they should be fulfilled, even if only to reinforce the efforts of the facilitation session participants.

B. Goals and Objectives to Set

Before initiating an action-item tracking scenario, be sure to check with the client that these items from the facilitation session(s) have the support of management. Often, short-term tactical plans made during a facilitation session will not reflect a full knowledge of the business—for example, an impending announcement of the company's acquisition. Therefore, the facilitation results should always be submitted to management for approval.

Action-item tracking should be included within the consulting team's responsibilities, since it will affect the client's long-term impression of the effectiveness of the engagement. If possible, this should be stated explicitly in the original consulting proposal; if this is not said by the client, it should still be performed as part of the engagement overhead. And, whenever possible, tracking should be used as a leverage point to seek further consulting opportunities. (See Sections III.4 and III.5.)

C. How to Achieve These Goals and Objectives

To ensure that commitments are fulfilled, the following steps will be necessary:

- During the facilitation session(s), make sure that all commitments are discussed openly. All ongoing commitments should be included within the meeting's structure and should be included in the session report(s).
- Ideally, all action items should be recorded on standardized planning forms, such as the Planning Form shown earlier in this book (Exhibit 2.4). These will set forth the item committed to, the persons responsible, the time window to complete, budget and skills required, and other critical factors.
- Tactical Planning Forms should be included in the session report(s).
- Tactical Planning Forms should be explicitly tracked to ensure that commitments are upheld. This can be done by client management or by individuals appointed during the facilitation sessions.
- At the time of submission of the client's report, a proposal should be submitted for tracking any continuing commitments made during the engagement.
- If possible, the original proposal to the client should include responsibility for the consulting team to ensure implementation of the agreed-upon action items.

These steps are needed not as an enforcement measure but to keep the facilitation session's commitments alive. No matter how strong the commitments made during facilitation sessions are, these meetings are a special circumstance for the individuals involved. Once the meeting is over, participants return to their normal business role with its normal responsibilities and conflicts. After a period of weeks, implementation may slow down and commitments weaken. Only a well-structured tracking and implementation approach will ensure completion of the short-term action items.

D. *Questions and Issues to Remember*

o First, ensure that management understands that the facilitation session(s) will develop specific ideas and action plans; then determine if the client wants the consulting team to track or otherwise ensure the completion of these commitments.

o Assuming that implementation of these plans is part of the consulting assignment, develop a tracking sheet or tactical planning form that is agreeable to management.

o During the facilitation session, make sure that all group commitments are reduced to writing and specifically agreed to by all those with responsibilities assigned.

o Include all on going commitments in the participants' report.

o Include a summary of all commitments, across all sessions, in the client's report at the end of the engagement. Ensure that management is agreement.

o Establish a tracking mechanism, with specific personnel assigned and meetings scheduled to assess implementation progress.

o Ensure that implementation meetings continue to be held until all action items are complete.

o Establish, if agreeable to the client, an incentive program that rewards the full implementation of items agreed upon during the facilitation sessions.

III.4 Establish Plans for Longer-term Items

A. *Topic Description*

Section III.3 discussed implementation of action items and short-term tactical plans. This section discusses the slightly different situation of long-term strategic plans.

There is a major organizational difference between these two categories: Strategic plans are typically the purpose of the facilitative engagement, even in the CSA methodology context. That is the justification for hiring consultants, gathering participants, and focusing the organization on these particular issues. Action items and stand-alone tactical plans—that is, tactical plans that are not part of a larger strategic plan—usually come from the discussion flow of the facilitation meeting. Often they are unexpected—a minor change in a departmental business process that may have a major effect, which was discovered during the group discussions. Finally, they are easily implemented, in most cases in a short time and with a small budget.

Ensuring that long-term strategies are implemented is a major undertaking and involves different approaches from short-term action items.

B. *Goals and Objectives to Set*

The first step regarding implementation starts at the very beginning of the client relationship: The proposal must be absolutely clear on whether the consulting team is responsible for implementation of the recommendations, for tracking of that implementation by client personnel, or for nothing more than conducting a strategic planning engagement.

The last choice, simply doing the research and facilitation sessions, is the least desirable since it gives up control of project success to other parties. Here the engagement team's knowledge and commitment to the best possible long-term strategies will be lost to the client organization once the final report is submitted. Therefore, to the greatest extent possible, proposals should include either project tracking or participation in the implementation of recommended strategies.

Once formally involved in the tracking or implementation of strategies, the outside consulting team has a dual responsibility:

- To facilitation session participants, to elicit the maximum information possible and help develop that information into long-term strategies
- To management, to ensure that the strategies are implemented

There should be no conflict between these roles, since they typically will occur sequentially: first developing a strategy through facilitation sessions, then implementing it. Therefore, the consulting team should be prepared to change its roles and responsibilities when the client report is submitted.

C. How to Achieve These Goals and Objectives

Although based on a longer-term horizon, many of the goals and objectives for long-term strategies are identical to those for short-term action items. Therefore, the following list is similar to that presented in Section III.3:

- First, determine if the client wants the consulting team to track or otherwise ensure the completion of the strategic plans.
- Assuming that implementation of these plans is part of the consulting assignment, develop a tracking form that is agreeable to management.
- During the facilitation session, make sure that all strategies are clearly defined at the highest level, and have action plans specified within each strategy that will support its success.
- Include all strategies and supporting action plans in the participants' report.
- Include a summary of all strategies and supporting action plans, across all sessions, in the client report's at the end of the engagement.

o Establish a tracking mechanism, with specific personnel assigned and meetings scheduled to assess implementation progress. Become involved with both the implementation team and tracking function, developing a copartnering relationship with client personnel.

o Ensure that implementation meetings continue to be held until strategies are fully implemented or are continuing along a successful implementation path with little doubt of their eventual success.

o Establish, if agreeable to the client, an incentive program that rewards the organization for the implementation of strategic change.

D. Questions and Issues to Remember

The following list also has similarities to that presented in Section III.3:

o First, ensure that management supports the engagement team's participation in the implementation and/or tracking of strategic plans.

o Assuming that implementation of these plans is part of the consulting assignment, develop a tracking methodology that is agreeable to management.

o During the facilitation session, make sure that all strategies are clearly defined, supported where possible by specific action plans, and developed with strong consensus by session participants.

o Include all such plans in the participants' report.

o Include a summary of all commitments, across all sessions, in the client's report at the end of the engagement. Ensure that management is in agreement.

o Implement the agreed project tracking methodology, with specific personnel assigned and meetings scheduled to assess implementation progress.

○ Ensure that implementation meetings continue to be held until all strategies and/or action plans are complete.

○ Establish, if agreeable to the client, an incentive program that rewards the organization for successful strategic change.

III.5 Review Engagement; Seek Additional Needs

A. Topic Description

Research has shown that setting appropriate expectations is critical in any service business. In the consulting field, client expectations are high and similar performance is expected. Therefore, any successful consulting engagement, facilitated or not, must include the determination of whether client expectations have been met.

Going beyond that basic minimum, it is highly recommended that client satisfaction meetings be held regularly during any lengthy consulting engagement. Such meetings will enable clients to express dissatisfaction early on, so that corrective action can be taken.

Client satisfaction does not result from engagements that fulfill their expectations. True satisfaction comes only when client expectations have been exceeded, and to a significant degree. Therefore, the consulting team should set *reasonable* expectations (i.e., not the highest possible ones) at the outset, reasonable goals to achieve and to allow room for exceeding client expectations. With this approach, the consulting team will be rewarded with ongoing work, on-time invoice payments, and a long-term consulting relationship.

B. Goals and Objectives to Set

At the end of an engagement, it is particularly important to understand the need for both "disengagement" and "reengagement":

Disengagement refers to the closing phases and responsibilities of any engagement:

- o Presenting results
- o Answering questions
- o Resolving issues arising from the engagement
- o Ensuring that all responsibilities have been fulfilled—in both the consultants' and the client's minds

Reengagement refers to the opening of new consulting opportunities, based on the work conducted in the now-complete engagement:

○ Implementation of strategies developed
○ Discovery of new problem areas, highlighted by the open discussions in the facilitation sessions
○ In a CSA engagement, initiating the business process improvements that were recommended by participants
○ Developing proposals for additional work to ensure successful organizational change

At a higher level, the consulting team's goals for the disengagement/reengagement process include:

○ Determination of any remaining client issues, which should be remedied immediately
○ Understanding the client's level of satisfaction and any underlying reasons that can help improve future engagements
○ Establishing a forum for the client to express satisfaction clearly to the consultants, which will give the consultants a base of favorable comments to use for references in the future—to this client and others
○ Promoting ongoing consulting services that will help the client realize maximum value from the engagement just completed

C. How to Achieve These Goals and Objectives

○ It is necessary to propose, plan for, and schedule client satisfaction meetings from the very beginning of the engagement. In the ideal case, these are held on a regular (e.g., monthly) basis. In the worst case, the client satisfaction meeting is held only once—at the end of a long and complex engagement. In the worst-case situation, of course, negative client comments will come at a time when the consultants are unable to remedy the problems raised.

o All meetings with the key client should be open and candid, both in regard to client personnel and the consulting team. When problems are raised, they should be responded to forthrightly. Finally, remedial action items must be completed promptly and successfully.

o If the final meeting or meetings of an engagement involve a group presentation to client management, it is preferable to conduct a short client satisfaction minifacilitation at the end of the presentation. This will give the management team an opportunity to speak out about problems, which typically are lessened in the clients' mind when discussed openly among colleagues. It will also give the consulting team an opportunity to show its facilitation skills again, including the use of voting technology to obtain numeric data on client satisfaction scores.

o At the end of these last meetings, after results have been presented and potential future needs have been discussed, clients should be asked for their continuing business. Many consultants forget to ask this, and leave significant future billings on the table.

D. Questions and Issues to Remember

o Has the engagement been fully disengaged? Are all responsibilities fulfilled, are all action items complete?

o Has the consulting team presented itself and its results in the best possible light?

o Has the client been interviewed to determine any remaining areas of perceived need?

o Has a formal client satisfaction meeting been held, either with the single key client or with a group of client management?

o Have all possible future opportunities to give service been presented to the client?

o Has the client been asked for continuing business?

APPENDIX B

Listing of Electronic Voting Systems

NOTES:

1. All wireless systems use the same Fleetwood transceiver hardware. Although the hardware is identical, each company has its own software implementation for voting functionality. Hardware can address up to 255 participants per computer, up to 6 computers (1,500+ participants) per channel. Although wired systems are more reliable in signal transmission, clients seem to prefer wireless models; therefore, test any wireless system for complete reception of all votes transmitted.

2. Individual scatter diagrams: These are anonymous displays of all individual votes, including the location of their average, without voter identities shown. A second scatter diagram display shows the average vote position for all, surrounded by the average voting position of every stakeholder group. (Under this terminology, the top-level map showing the voting average position of all issues is not termed a "scatter.") These diagrams are very useful for showing agreement, disagreement, confusion, and polarity; they are also useful to show the differing positions of the various stakeholder groups.

3. On-site training: Means an unlimited number of operators can be trained at the same price. However, the actual limit for such training is from 10 to 20 operators in a classroom, and probably closer to 10, from practical experience.

Name of Software & Source Company	Address & Telephone	Voting Flexibility	Vote Display	Demo-graphics	# of Dimensions	Statistical Analysis	Individual Scatter Diagrams	Ease of Use: Scale: 1–9; 1 = Easy 9 = Hard
CoNexus 2000 software, c/o Leadership 2000, Inc. *Meeting CoNexiom* module featured here; others available at $2,500 each	3333 N. 44th Street Phoenix, AZ 85018 602 852-0223 fax: 602 852-0232	Advanced	Advanced	Yes	Up to 5	Intermediate	Yes plus individual voter maps	2 Intuitive user interface
Sharpe Decisions 2000 by Sharpe Decisions, Inc.	101 Van Buren Street Kemptville, Ontario K0G1J0 613 258-7049 fax: 613 258-4651 www.sharpedecisions.com	Advanced	Advanced	Yes	Up to 4	Advanced	Yes	2 Intuitive user interface

Option Finder software, c/o Option Technologies, Inc. 389 West Second, Suite B Ogden, UT 84404 801 621-2500 fax: 801 621-4677	Advanced; *Agenda* feature helps guide facilitator	Advanced	Yes	1 or 2	Inter-mediate	Yes	7 Complex user interface
Quick Tally Interactive Systems 8444 Wilshire Blvd. Beverly Hills, CA 90211 213 653-5303 1 800 241-6963 fax: 213 653-2725	Basic *Note:* This voting hardware is compatible with other software, such as Fleetwood and Sharpe Decisions.	Basic	Yes	1	No	No	4 Semi-intuitive user interface
wInquiry software, c/o Audience Response Systems, Inc. 2148 North Cullen Avenue Evansville, IN 47715 812 479-7507 1-800-INVOLVE fax: 812 479-1057	Basic	Basic	Yes	1	No	No	Not tested

Index

Printed and bound by CPI Group (UK) Ltd, Croydon, CR0 4YY

23/04/2025

14660922-0004